THE MONEY $AVVY Student

ADAM CARROLL

Book Press™
publishing

Published in Des Moines, Iowa, by:

BookPress Publishing
P.O. Box 71532, Des Moines, IA 50325
www.BookPressPublishing.com

The following are all registered trademarks: Nike, CNN Money, Totino's, Top Ramen, Money Smart Week, Craigslist, NBA, Mercedes-Benz, Five Guys Burgers and Fries, Auntie Anne's, 24 Hour Fitness, UGG, Under Armour, North Face, Lululemon Athletica, eBay, The Home Depot, Dunkin' Donuts, Etsy, E*Trade, Netflix, Pocket Expense, Mint, Yodlee, YNAB, SmartyPig, Vanguard, M&M's, Nationwide, The College Board, Google, Kiwanis, Rotary, Jaycees, Lions Clubs, Optimist Club, Soroptimist Club, Knights of Columbus, CLEP, Starbucks, Khan Academy, Lynda.com, YouTube, Udemy, Udacity, edX, Coursera, Codecademy, Hershey's, John Deere, Google Places, Facebook, Twitter, Snapchat, Instagram, Amazon, Gumroad, PayPal, Shopify, MailChimp, WordPress, Canva, 99designs, Upwork, Kickstarter, Indiegogo, and GoFundMe.

Publisher's Cataloging-in-Publication Data

Names: Carroll, Adam Paul, author.
Title: The Money Savvy Student / Adam Carroll.
Description: Includes bibliographical references. | Des Moines, IA: BookPress Publishing, 2016.
Identifiers: ISBN 978-0-9905578-2-1 | LCCN 2016952454
Subjects: LCSH Youth--Finance, Personal. | Young adults--Finance, Personal. | Young adult consumers. | College students--United States--Finance, Personal. | BISAC BUSINESS & ECONOMICS / Personal Finance / Money Management |
Classification: LCC HG179 .C334 2016 | DDC 332.024/055--dc23

First Edition
Printed in the United States of America
10 9 8 7 6 5 4 3 2 1

This book is dedicated to the students of today who will someday reform the economy that's been perilously placed on their shoulders. I have tremendous hope for what you're able to accomplish.

To the teachers of today who encourage, prod, cajole, love, and in the end, bring out the best in our youth.

To my own Money Savvy Students—Piper, Nolan, and Davis. I love and appreciate each of you for the remarkable humans you are.

And to Jenn, I am eternally grateful for your support of the mission I'm on. I love you.

CONTENTS

ACKNOWLEDGMENTS

Writing a book like this is a task that requires a team of people in order for it to come to fruition. This wouldn't be in your hands if not for the following people to whom I'm deeply grateful for:

Anthony Paustian—Thank you for being a great friend, the most detail-oriented person I've ever wanted in my corner, and a persistent nag when I was behind. I owe you a great deal.

Sara Stibitz—You are a wordsmith and a bright light in the world. From you I learned that you have to first break things to create anew.

Mike Paustian—Design has got to be your middle name. Thanks for the continued refinements to the cover of this book and more to come.

My mastermind and accountability partners—Drew McLellan, Mitch Matthews, David Beebe, Jacob Kent, Joel Jackman, Anthony Paustian, Chad Carden, Tim Augustine, and Mike Wagner. I've never had a brother; I've always had many.

My family—Jenn, Piper, Nolan and Davis. Thanks for the understanding of time spent away from you to work on projects like this. I love you each so much and appreciate your support and encouragement daily.

Mom and Dad, Heather and Sherry, Jan and Hans—Your belief in me helps me to move ever closer to my goals.

Starbucks & Hy-Vee—Thanks for the coffee, the wi-fi, and for not kicking me out after four hours of taking up space multiple days a week.

INTRODUCTION

Here's a bold prediction. Reading this book will mark the beginning of a long and prosperous life, *if you take it seriously.*

Students everywhere are being introduced to this book, and some will think of it as more homework—just another 138 pages they have to finish before Friday. But, those who treat this book as their financial wake-up call will find that the pages hold more than stories and ideas to be more Money Savvy. This book contains fundamental, foundational wisdom that EVERY person must understand if they are to achieve financial success in their lives.

- If you're a part of a school system where personal finance is a required course, consider yourself lucky.

- If your parents are the kind of people who talk to you about money, consider yourself luckier.

- If, by chance, you've read other books on making, saving, managing, or investing money, you are WAY ahead of the game and this book will be a booster shot to your financial future. You can consider yourself the luckiest.

The majority of students today go through their secondary education years without ever learning the key foundational principles that are taught in the pages of *The Money Savvy Student*. Most of them pursue higher education, waste precious time and money in the process of "finding" themselves, and over-borrow on student loans to fund a four- to six-year party. They then graduate into a job that doesn't give them the life they imagined because they never imagined having tens of thousands of dollars of debt.

But not you. You're different. Because you hold this book in your hands and you intend to take it seriously, you're on a different path. The opportunity before you could be life-changing.

This book will guide you on that path, giving you an understanding of money and why it will play an integral part in your life as you progress through your teenage years, 20s, and beyond. It's possible for someone of modest income to reach financial independence by their 30s IF they apply Money Savvy principles. By the end of these 138 pages, you'll understand that money is as important or more so than reading, writing, and simple arithmetic.

The bottom line is that you'll use this information for the rest of your life. You'll read and write that long too, but being Money Savvy makes those things easier.

You'll notice as you read through the following chapters that the key elements, vocabulary, and ideas are **bolded**. You can glance through the book after reading through once and identify all the concepts that need to be reviewed.

The research and background for this book came from hundreds of conversations with students just like you. As a financial educator, over the past decade I've spoken to well over 250,000 people in college and high school audiences, spreading the message about how to be more Money Savvy. I've found there are three kinds of people in the crowd: students, tourists, and inmates.

- Students show up because they want to learn something from me.

- Tourists are there because they came with a friend or heard there was free food.

- Inmates are forced to be there, usually getting extra credit for showing up.

I hope you show up as a student while reading this book. I hope you understand the words on these pages were written by someone who cares deeply about your ability to achieve whatever you want in life. It's up to you to understand, to practice, and to live out the principles in this book and become the most Money Savvy Student you can be.

PART 1
The Foundation

Look up the word "foundation" in the dictionary and one of
the definitions is "an underlying basis or principle of something." Part One of *The Money Savvy Student* will provide
you with the underlying basis for which this book was
written, an understanding of why this information is important for you, and some suggestions on how best to apply the
following chapters to your life.

YOU ARE EXPENSIVE

One Monday morning in a classroom in an affluent Texas town, after settling the students down and handing them each a small spiral-bound notebook, the teacher asked each of the students to make a list of everything they wore that day.

The students gave vacant looks, trying to figure out what the teacher was up to. One student raised her hand and asked, "You want us to list our clothes?"

"Yes, we'll start with what you're wearing. And I want everything listed from your shoes and socks to your earrings." The teacher turned back to the papers on her desk as if to say, "Get to it."

The students listed their items of clothing in the spiral-bound notebooks—Nike tennis shoes, white socks, blue jeans, sweatshirt. About four minutes into the exercise, the teacher said, "Make sure you list *everything*—Underwear, belts, watches, necklaces, bras." At this point the guys pointed at each other and laughed.

Once the teacher settled down the juvenile humor, she asked them to add to the list any surgeries like getting tonsils or an appendix removed, any dental work like fillings or crowns, any orthodontics like braces or headgear, if they wore glasses or contacts, or if they ever had corrective devices like knee braces. She told them to write those down below the list of clothing they wore that day.

Once everyone stopped writing, the teacher then turned to athletics, music, and other extra-curricular activities. "Below your braces and glasses, list the sports you're involved in, musical instruments you play, and any other activity you might be in like drama or debate."

By this point, the students were curious about the teacher's angle and were making guesses about the purpose of the exercise. One of the students chimed in with, "I suppose you'll want what we ate for breakfast next."

"Exactly," was the teacher's response. "And what you typically have for lunch and dinner on an ordinary day."

Most of the class thought this was an exercise meant to waste a portion of class. However, the teacher had other plans.

"By now you should have a long list of things you're wearing, procedures you've undergone, activities you're a part of, and food you might eat on any given day," she told them. "The next step is to put a retail price on everything. Next to your list, I want you to write a *realistic* price you'd pay for what you're wearing, what your braces cost, how much your activities are, and how much your food costs. If you need help assigning a price to your items, just work with the people around you. Oh, and we'll be doing this exercise every day for the next week."

As you might expect, there was a bit of grumbling about the fact they'd have to do this exercise every day, and one student asked, "I'm fine with recording all of this if you will tell us what the point is?"

"The point," the teacher said dryly, "is to establish the fact that **YOU ARE EXPENSIVE.**"

For an entire week, the students in this Texas class carried around a small spiral-bound notebook and documented the clothing they wore each day, the food they ate, the activities in which they participated, the gas they consumed, and the cell phone bill attached to their phones. Every expense that might be incurred on their behalf went into the notebook, even if it was questionable.

At the end of the week, the students tallied up how much they cost their parents for that week. The results ranged from a few hundred dollars to thousands of dollars, and when cars, phones, camps, and vacations were added, the numbers jumped to tens of thousands.

According to *CNN Money*, the average cost to raise a child from birth to 18 is $245,000.[1] To deliver a baby at a hospital today has a price tag between $20,000 and $50,000 (health insurance usually covers some of this)—kind of makes that one week look like chump change, doesn't it?

Let's take it one step further…

For your parents to fork out the full $245,000 in after-tax dollars, they would have to make 30-40% more than that before income taxes are taken out. That means the total amount of income needed to raise you from age zero to 18 is closer to $325,000. No wonder they feed you Totino's Party Pizzas and Top Ramen.

See for Yourself....

1. Take a personal inventory of what you're currently wearing and assign a retail value to it. Be sure to include everything from top to bottom.

2. Next, add up all the surgeries, dental work, orthodontia, glasses or contacts, etc.

3. Now, estimate the cost of your extracurricular activities, camps, etc.

4. Finally, estimate how much you consume in food on a daily basis.

Add all of these figures up to get a sense of how much you cost your parents. Keep in mind this is ONE DAY (granted, we're including things like braces, glasses, and extra-curriculars, but you get the point). If you add in your phone service, your car payments and/or insurance, and anything else covered by Mom and Dad, you should feel compelled to give them a big hug when you see them next.

The point of this story and the exercise above is not to make you feel guilty nor to make you swear off lunch and wear a garbage bag to school to save a buck. The point is to illustrate that even though you may not be aware of it, it costs

A LOT of money to live. Even as a student, there is a significant cost to living your life.

For a majority of students, their parents cover the bulk of their daily expenses. When you have no awareness of how much was spent to make you look as good as you do, you might assume it's a small amount. As you have now learned, that is not so.

Realizing that life is expensive is a central principle for the Money Savvy Student. Your understanding of the costs associated with progressing toward adulthood will help you make some very important decisions in the near future. The expenses you'll incur from this point forward will only grow—they rarely shrink.

Do yourself a favor and thank your parents tonight for working so hard on your behalf. They'll probably fall off their chairs at dinner. It'll be awesome.

YOUR FINANCIAL SUCCESS IS ENTIRELY UP TO YOU

Carlos was a college student who approached me at a university event. He had waited around for quite some time to chat with me and I could tell he was eager to share his story. After exchanging names and some pleasantries, I asked him what he took away from my presentation.

"Basically, I learned that I've been doing the right things for quite some time," was his reply.

"That's great to hear, Carlos. Where and how did you learn about money?" I asked.

"I would say from my parents, but ultimately it was on my own. When I was 15, my Dad sat me down and told me they'd give me food, shelter, and $50 a month, but the rest was up to me."

He piqued my curiosity, so I asked him, "What do you mean the rest was up to you?"

"Toiletries, gas, cell phone, entertainment, school clothes, and supplies. Basically, everything that a kid needs to get through high school I had to purchase myself."

"Wow," I said, "What was that like?"

"It was brutal. I hated my parents for about a year because of it. I couldn't understand why all the other kids I went to school with got everything handed to them, but I had to make drastic choices just to cover the necessities," he said.

"What happened after that first year?" I asked. "And how is the relationship with your parents now?"

"It's great. It took time to realize they were preparing me for the decisions I'd have to make as an adult, but they were doing it while I was still under their protection. After getting over being angry, I noticed my friends were wearing the same clothes as me, but they'd paid retail and I was buying the clothes second-hand. They would trash their cars or their phones and think nothing of it. It became obvious they were making stupid decisions with money because it wasn't their money—it was their parents' money," he explained.

Carlos was a first generation American citizen; his parents had immigrated from Cuba when Carlos was just a baby. His parents were hard-working, blue-collar employees who wanted to instill in Carlos a sense of identity and the same work ethic they had. As a result, they financially "cut loose" every child in their home at the age of 15, providing necessities like food and shelter, and supplying them $50 to pay for their needs. They had to budget or work for anything over and above the $50. They were there to help them make the best decisions.

When Carlos and I met, he was 20 years old and had spent the first two years of his college career at a community college, acquiring his Associate's Degree and working part-time so he didn't have to take on any loans. He saved nearly $20,000 on his own during high school by working part-time and doing side-hustles to make extra money. He intended to use that to pay for his time at a state university. However, due to Carlos's work ethic and intense value of money, he applied to dozens of scholarships to help cover the cost of the last two years of his undergraduate degree.

Carlos is off to an incredibly Money Savvy start thanks to his parents' brave decision to equip their child with just enough money to make him choose wisely.

How Much Would You Need?

Most students don't pay much attention to how much money they need on a weekly basis because their parents are taking care of all the costs. However, if YOU were in Carlos's situation, how much would you need?

When you added up how expensive you are in Chapter One, were you surprised at the number? Did it make you think twice about spending on clothes or technology (even if it's your parents' money)? What would you need to do to reduce spending if it were all on you?

The last question is the most important to think through, even if it's just an exercise. Many recent college graduates (actually, we could assume *most* college graduates) ask themselves where they need to cut back spending once they get their first paychecks. Because it's their first time thinking through this dilemma, many find it hard to get their expenses down to a manageable level. By walking through the thought process now, you'll be better prepared when you're out on your own.

The most logical things to cut back on are food, clothing, vehicle payments, and rent. What are five other ways to cut your spending so you can afford yourself?

1.
2.
3.
4.
5.

Here's a hint: Most people spend much more than they intend on luxuries and conveniences. Luxuries would be things you can do without but enjoy having in your life. That may include things like jewelry, watches, expensive clothing, meals out, etc. Convenience items are things that are bought in the moment because they're very convenient. Grabbing something to eat at a gas station would be a convenience expense. Buying coffee could be both a luxury AND a convenience item. If you're having a hard time figuring out how to cut back, start in these categories!

Carlos's parents did what your parents will someday want to do—cut you off. Pay close attention to the next statement because it's a big factor to your financial success in life.

Your Parents Don't Want to Support You Forever.

You've already read how much you cost your parents up to the age of 18. If your parents are offering to cover a portion or all of your college costs, tack on another $80-$250K to the amount on page seven. Trust me, at some point they want you off the payroll.

There will come a time when your parents once and for all tell you they're done supporting you. It shouldn't come as a surprise. In fact, you can bet it will suck for a while, but the lessons you'll learn will be invaluable. For some, that might happen at age 18, while others might not get cut off until the age of 21 to 23. If you're in a family like Carlos's, it might be closer to 15. Just know that whenever it happens, it's part of the natural order of life. Your grandparents couldn't wait to get your parents out of the house and out of their wallets—ask them.

As a Money Savvy Student, you have options. You can:

1. Ride your parents' gravy train, assuming it will never stop, and be blindsided when they take away your parental ATM.

2. Or, you can learn what you need to learn about Savvy money management now—while enjoying the benefits of the gravy train—and be ready to step off when asked.

Option one will be like walking into a full-on Category Five hurricane with no umbrella, no rain coat, and nothing to hold onto for safety.

Option two will be like learning how to swim. You'll move from the shallow end while treading water and learning to hold your breath, to putting your face underwater and holding your breath, to learning strokes and kicks to keep you afloat, to diving off the diving board into the deep end, all the while knowing you're safe.

Which would you prefer? I encourage you to view Option two as a tremendous opportunity to prepare yourself for a life of financial abundance and prosperity.

I met Jerry, the father of twin daughters, at a Money Smart Week event I hosted in conjunction with a local credit union. The program I delivered was called *Unplugging The Parental ATM*, and I was sharing strategies with parents on how to teach effective money management to their children as young as five and as old as 35. Believe it or not, there are a crazy amount of people in their 20s, 30s, and 40s who still rely on their parents for money!

Jerry looked seriously concerned as I talked through ideas on how to impart Money Savvy principles to children, and at one point I said, "You have a really odd look on your face as I'm talking about this. Is everything okay?"

Jerry told me about his twin daughters who were attending community college in Los Angeles, California. They were aspiring actresses and had moved to be close to the action and to work on getting their degrees, but it seemed they were more intent on working on their tans.

"What do you do when your kids text you about putting more money in their accounts?" Jerry asked.

"How often is it happening?" I asked.

"Every other week, sometimes every week. We put enough in their account to last them a full two weeks or more, but it seems they're spending money in places they shouldn't. When the rent, phone, or cable bill comes due, they ask for more. My wife just ignores the texts, so now they text me."

"What do *you* do?" I asked.

"Well, I put more into their accounts because I don't want them to struggle," Jerry answered.

At this point, I looked around the room to all the other parents and asked them, "Did *you* struggle when you were 20?" Every one of them nodded their heads in agreement.

Jerry's daughters didn't understand that their parents didn't want to support them forever. In fact, because Jerry put money in every time they texted, they probably believed they *would* be supported forever. As a result, there was no motivation to learn how to manage the money better. The only thing they knew for certain was that if they were close to running out of funds, they had better text Daddy.

The hard reality of this family's situation is that none of them are benefiting. Jerry feels used by his girls because they view him as a money fountain and the girls are learning nothing about living on their own. If nothing changes, the girls will continue to ask their parents for money well into their 20s and 30s.

While this may not seem like a big deal, most parents in this situation aren't saving enough for their own retirement. Some aren't able to save *anything* for retirement. The flip side for Jerry's daughters is they may be financially supporting their parents when they become too old to work and don't have enough money to support themselves.

Money Savvy Students understand **their parents don't want to support them forever** and prepare themselves for a life of making Savvy decisions, regardless of how much their parents support them financially. They are also grateful for the funding and support given by parents while it's there instead of being frustrated when it's not.

When you understand that your financial well-being is entirely up to you, you'll get serious about educating yourself, make Money Savvy decisions, and live a life of financial security, contentment, and abundance.

A SIMPLE CONCEPT

When Income Exceeds Expenses, that's Good.
When Expenses Exceed Income, that's Bad.

While this concept may seem simple to you, knowing the number of people who don't understand this would blow your mind.

When I speak to groups of students, I always ask this question: What is four minus five?

If you answered negative one, then congratulations, you've been paying attention in math. For such a simple concept learned in elementary school, there is a huge percentage of adults in this country who might make $4,000 a month and spend $5,000 and think nothing of it. People who live this way are deeply in debt, rarely save and invest, and more than likely are rather miserable under the stress.

Let's bring this down to a student level. If you work a part-time job at $9 an hour and work ten hours a week, you would make $90 a week before taxes are taken out. That means that over the course of a four-week month, you'd make $360. (In this example, let's assume you have no taxes taken out of your paycheck.)

If you spend $300 of your income that month in expenses and have $60 left, that's good.

If you spend $400 of your income that month in expenses, you'd either be dipping into savings, "borrowing" from Mom and Dad, or putting $40 on a credit card. That's bad.

Another way to look at your personal finances is by viewing what you do as "Company YOU." If you were to invest in the stock market, putting the money in "Company YOU" (CY), you'd want to make sure the company is profitable, making it a good investment.

A profitable company is one where the income or revenue is greater than the expenses. When CY's revenue is greater than expenses, the company is profitable because there is money left at the end of the month or the year. Profitable companies are better than unprofitable ones because they work hard at keeping their revenue (income) high and their expenses low.

The same is true of families. A family that has money left at the end of the month would be considered a profitable family. One that spends everything they make and then some would be unprofitable.

This is also true of students. A student working part-time who has money left over at the end of the month would be profitable. A student who spends all the money they make every single week and has nothing left to show for it at the end of the month is not profitable.

So, given your particular financial situation, would YOU invest in Company YOU?

My boys are into basketball in a BIG way and love watching the NBA. This drives my wife nuts because she was known for her defensive skills in high school basketball, and NBA players are notorious for rarely playing defense. While the score of the games might get well above 100 points, the players are mainly playing offense.

To win ANY game, including the game we all play with money, you have to be good at both offense AND defense. **Offense is your ability to make money.** I'll go through some ideas on how you can make money as a Money Savvy Student toward the end of the book. Obviously, getting a degree, starting a business, learning a trade, and hard work can go into making money. However, there are many factors that go into your ability to make a living.

The first thing to consider is this—are you entrepreneurial or would you be more inclined to go look for a job? Each has its own pros and cons, and it's entirely possible to have a job AND be entrepreneurial as well. As a general rule, *someone who is more entrepreneurial is probably going to make more money per hour than someone who works a part-time job.* As an example, let's say you can make $9 an hour at a part-time job, but you could make $45 mowing lawns. Assuming a lawn takes you one hour to mow, you'd have to work five hours at your part-time job to make the same amount of money (and we're not factoring taxes into the equation).

To play great offense, realizing where you can add value is key. If, let's say, you preferred working a part-time job, how could you add value to the work you do so your employer is more likely to pay you more? The ability to make money and play great offense is fairly simple—continually add more value than what you're paid to do. As your hard work, effort, creativity, and attitude are noticed, your paycheck will increase.

I met a young man named Frank while he was doing some work on a property I own. Frank had gone to a technical school to learn welding and was hired full-time by a large tractor company in the Midwest. He'd been there about 6 years, and about once a year, Frank and his fellow welders were laid-off for a short time. During this time he posted ads on Craigslist for painting and light maintenance. I had hired him to do a simple paint job and Frank went above and beyond my expectations. When I asked him why he did this work, he shared that he was currently getting his Masters degree in psychology and would eventually pursue a doctorate. Doing welding and other odd jobs allowed him to make great money while not being too mentally taxing so he could study in his off hours.

Frank is an example of someone playing great offense. Not only was he an employee AND an entrepreneur, he was a student looking to increase the value of his time.

Defense is your ability to keep expenses low. You can take this to an extreme by living off the grid, extreme couponing, living in a tiny house, dumpster diving, etc. However, keeping expenses low could also mean driving a used car when you really want a new one, canceling your cable subscription at home, buying clothes secondhand, and making your lunch every day. Reality television showcases the "extreme" savers, but being Money Savvy is about making smaller, more significant decisions on a daily basis.

Professional athletes are notoriously good at making money, and notoriously bad at keeping expenses low. Take Shaquille O'Neal as an example. When Shaquille O'Neal signed his first NBA contract, he reportedly spent $1,000,000 in 45 minutes. He bought his parents a home and a Mercedes-Benz for each of them, as well as a Benz for himself. Great offense, terrible defense.

Fortunately, Shaq had a banker who was looking out for his best interests. The banker called Shaq and told him that unless he wanted to end up like all the other broke former professional athletes in the world, he better put 75% of his income away and live on 25% (still an enormous sum of money). Shaq listened to his banker, then became an educated Money Savvy basketball player. While playing in the NBA, Shaq pursued his bachelor's degree, his M.B.A., and an Ed.D. (a Doctorate in Education).

Today, Dr. Shaquille O'Neal jointly owns 155 Five Guys Burgers and Fries franchises, 17 Auntie Anne's pretzel restaurants, 150 car washes, 40 24 Hour Fitness centers, a shopping center, a movie theater, and several Las Vegas nightclubs.[1]

While defense is not the biggest part of Shaq's game (on or off the court), his ability to keep expenses low allowed him to expand his offense (making money). (Shaq more than likely surrounded himself with a team of great advisors, attorneys, and accountants as well!)

The single best way to get in the habit of making sure your expenses are less than your income is to follow the advice from the book *The Richest Man in Babylon* by George S. Clason. In this classic financial education book written in 1926, Clason describes the Richest Man in Babylon building his wealth through several habits, the first of which is that **10% of all you make is yours to keep.**

Now, you may think, "Well of course 10% is mine to keep. One hundred percent of my paycheck is mine to keep." For most students, when you have money in your pocket it gets spent. **The 10% that Clason writes about is money that is kept. It's not spent but rather saved for future use, investing, and building wealth.**

When 10% of all the money you make is set aside, it takes on a life of its own. The first few weeks of taking this money out of your paycheck may seem painful, but once the balance grows, you'll feel the emotional rewards of forming this incredible habit. Once the habit is set, you won't think twice about putting that money aside.

It's critical that you learn and practice this habit now while your income is low. It is far easier to put away $36 from the $360 you made in one month than it will be to put away $360 from the $3,600 you'll make each month in the next few years or the $3,600 from the $36,000 you'll make each month later in your career (if you put your mind to it, it's possible!).

Once the habit is set, the amount of money you're

making and saving is irrelevant. At that point, it's the behavior of setting money aside that makes you Money Savvy.

YOUR FRIENDS AND FAMILY INFLUENCE YOUR FINANCIAL VALUES

Your Family...

Whether your parents know it or not, they've been teaching you about money since you were a small child.

- When they paid with cash or a credit card, you were consciously or unconsciously recording that moment in time and assigning a meaning to it.

- When they told you, "We can't afford that," or "Money doesn't grow on trees," they were imprinting a financial script in your mind you've been running ever since.

- When you overheard an argument about something money related, you subconsciously attached money and conflict.

- When your dad said, "I don't have cash, ask your mother," you made a connection that men don't have money but women do (or vice versa depending on the conversation).

This is not meant to be a slam on your parents—their parents did the exact same thing, which is why they are now sharing the same tidbits of wisdom with you. We keep passing the same faulty money programming down through the generations.

The messages we hear often stick with us, unbeknownst to us, running in the background whenever we're about to make a decision concerning money. Have you ever heard any of the following statements?

"I'm not made of money."

"Money is hard to come by."

"You have to work hard for money."

"We're always broke."

"Money doesn't buy happiness."

"Only rich people have those."

"We can't afford that."

In contrast, some of the positive, affirming statements you might hear are:

"We save for the future."

"We are choosing not to buy that right now."

"Stuff is fine but experiences are better."

"That's not in our budget right now."

The negative statements are the result of money programming handed down from your grandparents to your parents, and they probably don't know the effect it's having on them and on you. The key is to reframe the statement in a more positive, controllable, affirming way when you hear any of these statements.

For example, if you hear someone say, "We can't afford that," it suggests the control lies somewhere else. Subconsciously, it pushes the ability to afford it away because you have no control in the statement. Instead, reframe the statement to, "We choose not to buy that right now. Our money is better used elsewhere." **Choosing allows you to stay in control, while defaulting to "We can't" or "I can't" statements takes away your power over the money you do have.**

Over the next couple of weeks, pay close attention to the comments your parents make when paying bills, grocery shopping, saving for a vacation, etc. Once you are aware of conscious and unconscious messages they're sending, you'll be able to filter out the messages that don't support the financial life you'd like to have.

Just a small tweak from "We can't afford it," to "That's not in our budget right now," has a very profound financial meaning. One takes the power away while the other suggests that you save for things you want as part of your budget. The second statement is very Money Savvy.

Your Friends...

Your friends are influencing your money beliefs and values as well. If your friends are all wearing name brand apparel (think Nike, UGG boots, Under Armour, North Face, Lululemon, etc.), most students, in a desire to fit in, will also lean toward those name brands. If your parents are buying school clothes for you and you want name brands, you might hear the comments above because they were told the same things growing up. In this instance, your friends are influencing the behavior of higher spending on clothes.

That doesn't mean they always have to be a bad influence on spending behavior. A group of friends came to me after an event and told me they were positive influences on each other when it came to spending on clothes. They called themselves the Budget Brigade and told me about their "shopping parties," where they would define a set amount of money to take to the mall. Armed with the same amount, each of them would go from store to store looking for the best deals on the cutest outfits. At the end of the shopping party, they'd meet back at someone's house and compare how little they'd spent and show off what they'd purchased. They told me that shopping for bargains was more fun (and took more time) than just running in and blowing money at stores. They even kept track of the outfits they really liked and let each other know when something went on sale.

A student I met in an East Coast high school told me she and her friends love to go to the movies together. As someone raised in a Money Savvy home, she would often buy candy for one dollar and keep it in her purse, while her friends would pay full movie theater price for candy (sometimes four or five times the amount for the same thing). Her friends gave her grief for it until they realized she always had extra money while they blew their entire allowance on movie tickets and candy.

You've no doubt heard the phrase "Keeping Up with the Joneses," which describes the idea of spending money to keep up the same living standard as their peers. This is just as prevalent among students as it is among adults. As an example, a young woman named Erin had a college roommate named Lauren who suggested they go out to eat A LOT, and often chose more expensive restaurants. Erin went along on the dinner outings because she wanted to fit in, and was concerned she wouldn't be included if she chose not to go. The problem was that her credit card balance was ballooning from all of the restaurant tabs while she still paid for a dining center plan. Lauren's parents paid off her credit card every month and rarely questioned the charges. In an effort to "keep up" with Lauren, Erin was getting in a bigger financial bind every month.

When "Keeping Up with the Joneses" as a student, the difference is most students are attempting to keep up with the spending of their peers' *parents*, which varies greatly depending on the family income and how much financial help the student is getting. The solution here is simple: know your budget inside and out, and if you want to do more of what your peers are doing, figure out how to play offense and defense that much better.

PART 2
The Basics

Warren Buffett, one of the richest men in the world, is not just a Savvy investor; he understands the basics better than just about everyone. Buffett started his fortune at the young age of eight when he saved the income he was making as a paperboy. He later hired multiple friends to deliver papers along his ever-expanding route, and invested those funds into pinball machines, which he placed in barber shops all over the city. Even as a student, Warren understood the basics of being Money Savvy: income, savings, investments, low expenses, and continual education.

At the core of being a Money Savvy Student are the basics, the foundational building blocks of your life as they pertain to money. This section will give you the information you need to grow your ability to make, save, manage, and invest money. There will be a focus on the vocabulary used to be Money Savvy in Part Two with a focus on how to use that vocabulary to increase your income and Money Savvy-ness in Part Three.

INCOME

In this chapter we'll explore the various kinds of income, what you're trading income for, and how to think in different ways about the income you're either making or will eventually make.

The reason you're in school, and will potentially go to college, the trades, or the military, is to learn how to do something in exchange for money. **That *something* you're trading for money is time or expertise.**

At a barbecue restaurant in Kansas City, they have a sign on the door that says:

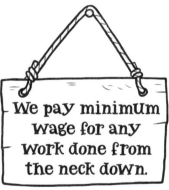

We pay minimum wage for any work done from the neck down.

In other words, if you have a substantial amount of thinking involved in your job, then you're likely paid more for it. If there is limited thinking, then you're most likely doing work from the neck down. Your time, therefore, is not worth as much as someone who's doing more thinking. This is the primary reason students are encouraged to further their schooling—when you are educated in a certain topic, industry, or major, your time becomes more valuable because you'll be doing far more thinking in your career.

If your goal is to make more income, the focus should be on increasing the value of your time. By taking jobs that require more thought, by educating yourself in particular specialties, or by mastering certain skills, you'll make your time more valuable and increase your potential income exponentially.

Types of Income

There are various types of income. **The most common form of income is earned income or W-2 income.** W-2 income is income earned in a job where your employer will automatically take taxes out of your paycheck and submit those to Uncle Sam—both the state and federal government. If you have a part-time job and you're surprised when you get your check because it's less than what you thought it would be, you're in a W-2 income job.

The term W-2 refers to the tax form you'll receive in January every year detailing how much gross income (the total amount) you made from the year before, how much was deducted for Federal and State taxes, and any other withhold-ings. We'll cover taxes in a later section, but for now under-stand that your income taxes help pay for our American government system.

In addition to taxes taken out of your paycheck, you'll notice additional amounts deducted for social security, and potentially insurance and retirement. Once you're working full-time, your employer will most likely cover a portion of your health insurance. The remaining balance will be covered by you and taken automatically from your paycheck. Your retirement contributions go into a 401k or 403b (retirement account), and are meant to help you achieve a comfortable retirement sometime in the future.

Another type of income is 1099 income. This is money you make as an independent contractor or self-employed person. 1099 income is different from W-2 income because taxes are not taken out of a 1099 paycheck.

This has both pros and cons to it. In the "pro" column, because there are no taxes taken out, your paycheck is bigger. If you're paid $15 an hour as a contractor and you work 10 hours, your paycheck would be $150. In the "con" column, because taxes are not taken out, you'll owe money at tax time, so holding money in reserve (usually 20% to 30%) is a good idea. The best way to do this is to set up an additional savings account for the payment of taxes at the end of the year. Auto-matically transfer 20-30% from your check into this account. If you end up owing less at the end of the tax year, congrat-ulations, you've come out ahead!

To put the two types of income into perspective, the

following scenarios are from real-life students working in jobs; some earn a paycheck, while others earn money as a self-employed person:

Rachel works for a retail store making $9.50 an hour. She works between 10-15 hours a week. Her employer takes taxes out of her paycheck and submits them to the IRS on her behalf. Rachel is making W-2 income.

David works at a restaurant as a waiter. He makes $4.25 an hour plus tips. David can work as much or as little as he likes based on his academic and sports schedule. Some weeks he works as many as 20 hours, some weeks as little as five hours. David's paycheck varies based on his hours and his tips. His employer takes taxes out of his paycheck and submits them to the IRS on his behalf. David is making W-2 income.

Piper walks dogs in her neighborhood. Over the past three years in high school, she's built an established clientele who trust her with their dogs. She charges $20 a week for a 20 to 30 minute walk every day, five days a week. Piper can handle walking five dogs at a time and has 15 clients paying her weekly. She even set up an automatic payment plan for them on PayPal so she doesn't have to collect the money. Piper is making 1099 income.

Caleb works for a contractor in the afternoon and on

the weekends delivering materials to job sites on an as-needed basis. The contractor has a small crew and needs all of them on-hand to work; having Caleb as a runner makes his crew more efficient. Caleb receives $11 an hour for the work he does. His workload varies based on how busy the crew is during the week. The contractor pays Caleb without taking taxes out. Caleb is making 1099 income.

Within the next decade, it's predicted that nearly 50% of our working population will be composed of independent contractors working for 1099 income.[1] Due to the Internet creating a global workforce willing to work on a project basis, Americans and American companies are following suit. Mastering one skill, service, or area of expertise will become more and more financially fruitful. You'll find that if you are an excellent graphic designer, writer, editor, video production specialist, or welder (among hundreds of other professions), there will be mass amounts of work on a project-by-project basis.

Understanding how to function in a more entrepreneurial environment will become increasingly important. As more and more companies hire contractors to do the work that employees used to do, your ability to "run your own business" by offering specific services is a huge advantage. We'll discuss ideas on how to do this in Part Three.

There are three other forms of income that aren't talked about much at your age, but if you understand them, it can help set you up for financial success and freedom much earlier than normal. *These three forms of income are: passive, portfolio, and rental.*

Passive income is income you make on a monthly, quarterly, or annual basis that you don't have to "work" for. The idea behind passive income is you're not trading time for money, but instead you've invested time and money into something so it generates cash flow on a regular basis.

To illustrate passive income at a level a student could understand (and participate in), I invested in gumball machines to see what kind of return could be expected. With $350 to invest, I searched eBay for gumball machines for sale and found two 4.5 feet tall machines from a seller a couple states away.

The seller was asking $125 per machine with $50 in shipping costs. Two machines, plus their shipping fees, cost $300, and two boxes of gumballs added another $50. All together, the total investment in my "business" was $350.

When the boxes arrived, I was ecstatic. As I tore into the packaging and pulled out the components of the gumball machines, my wife commented that I was like a kid on Christmas morning. The machines had bright red bases with an acrylic top and were shipped in pieces with some assembly required. After one trip to The Home Depot to purchase a pop rivet gun and about 30 minutes of figuring out the mechanics, I was in business.

Excited to see what kind of return I could generate, I placed the two machines with a local t-shirt shop owner who had retail stores in two separate shopping malls. I told the owners I was doing an experiment with the machines that would probably last about 12 months. My assumption was the two machines would generate around $20-$25 a month in passive income. They agreed to keep the machines right up front, close to the door.

You can imagine my surprise when I went in to collect the money after the first month and, between the two machines, there was $97 in quarters! I made almost a third of the money I invested in the business in the first month. Over the course of 12 months I made nearly $1,400 in passive income with an initial investment of only $350.

My daughter was around five years old when I did this experiment, and once a month we had a daddy/daughter Saturday where we went to Dunkin' Donuts, then went and collected quarters. As my daughter got in the car after polishing off a sprinkled cake doughnut, I asked her, "Where are we going today, sweetie?" Her answer? "To collect passive income, Daddy!" (At the age of five!)

I've told this story to hundreds of high school and college audiences, and inevitably someone will email me afterwards telling me they've purchased one, two, or in one case 15(!) gumball machines to place around their community. This is a passive income business that *anyone* can do with very minimal start-up costs. The biggest benefit is not trading time for money!

I shared this story with a teenaged student named Maddie who was already on an entrepreneurial path of her own when she bought her first machine. Maddie came to me after an event and told me she was inspired by the gumball machine story. For the previous couple of years she had been making hair bows and selling them at farmers' markets and on Etsy.com. She said, "Customers will walk up, look at my bows, turn around, and leave. Now, I have a way of collecting *something* from them before they leave. Everyone loves gumballs, especially kids, and there are almost always kids in tow."

Less than two weeks later I received an email from Maddie's mom. Not only had Maddie taken action on her decision to get a gumball machine, she had bought a jumbo machine and had her Trizzy Bows logo put on the front with a vinyl sticker. You can imagine my surprise when I found out that Maddie had her very own logo'd gumball machine *and* ran her Trizzy Bows business out of a trailer they pulled to the events. Today, her online and web sales make up a large portion of Maddie's business and the quarters for gumballs are a nice extra at local events. She's found it's a great draw to her booth for kids and parents alike.

Portfolio income is made from investing in stocks, bonds, mutual funds, or other products like real estate investment trusts (REITs). The main misconception among students is thinking they don't have enough money to invest to make portfolio income. Not true!

As of the writing of this book, my kids—ages 8, 11, and 13—all make portfolio income on a quarterly or annual basis. I'll first share why this happened and then share how they do it.

About a year ago, we decided as a family we would

implement an allowance program for the kids that amounted to one dollar per week for every year they've celebrated a birthday. At 10, they get $10 per week. At 11, $11. The kids are required to put 10% into long term savings, 10% towards charitable giving, and 10% into investing. This is a fairly standard budgeting philosophy called the 10/10/10/70 Plan. Every Saturday when they receive their allowance, they divide up the amounts and place the cash into glass jars labeled Give, Save, and Invest. The remaining 70% is theirs to spend however they choose.

We've found that forming the habits of saving for long-term goals, investing for the future, and charitable giving is common among nearly every affluent family in the country. Ten percent towards each is a common suggestion, though I encourage you to set your own amounts that help you reach your goals.

My very Savvy daughter has wanted to make money

for a long time—probably since collecting passive income from the gumball machines. When she received her weekly allowance, she asked me how she could make money from what she had in her save and invest jars. We talked about putting the money she collected once a month or once a quarter into a dividend paying stock. **A dividend paying stock is a share of a well-established, financially stable company that rewards shareholders with a payment every month, quarter, or year based on the number of shares owned.** When she found out she could buy shares of her favorite chocolate company (Hershey's–HSY) and get paid for owning shares, she was hooked.

Today, all three kids have a growing investment portfolio that includes dividend paying stocks and real estate investment trusts (which are funds that invest in real estate and pay a monthly dividend to the shareholders).

When the amount of money in their invest jar is sufficient to invest (usually $25 to $100), we login to their accounts on ETrade.com and purchase a quantity of shares in their chosen companies. All three like to check on the progress of their stocks on a semi-regular basis and know that if they continue investing like this over the next 20 years, they will be very wealthy later in life.

You will read more about investments later on in this book, but if you're interested in doing a deep dive into the topic, consider reading either *A Random Walk Down Wall Street* by Burton Malkiel, or *Rule One Investing* by Phil Town. Both were game-changers for me when it came to investing in the stock market.

The final type of income is rental income. **Rental income is income earned from the ownership of real estate.** While this is a tad more complicated than the previous two forms of income listed, it's still possible for a student to engage in rental income with the proper advice, partners, and mentorship.

Securing rental income involves purchasing a home, condo, duplex, fourplex, or apartment building and renting the space out to tenants. The tenants pay rent or a monthly fee to live in the property. Their rent typically covers the mortgage payment on the property plus any additional expenses that may be incurred on a monthly basis. The difference between the rent you receive and the expenses you have is rental income.

There are several advantages to investing in real estate and having rental income:

1. *Properties will generally increase in value.* Over time, the difference between what you paid for the property and what the property is worth will grow. If you bought the property at a good price, you may also have instant equity (or value in the property over and above the purchase price).

2. *Income is consistent when rented.* Part of the contract you have with your tenants is they can't stay if they don't pay. Because people need a place to live, having tenants in your property means you'll be getting a check every month.

3. *Your tenants are paying off your mortgage.* The

power of owning rental real estate isn't always in the monthly rental income, but in the fact that your tenants are paying off your mortgage, not you. The longer you hold the mortgage and own the property, the more this is true.

When I started investing in rental real estate at the age of 25, I had a challenge. I didn't have enough set aside to put a sufficient down payment on the property I wanted to buy. At the time, a down payment of at least 15% was required and the duplex I was looking at was listed at $112,000. That means I needed at least $16,800 at the time of the sale of the property. The duplex had been taken back by the bank from the previous owner in a foreclosure proceeding. Foreclosure is the result of someone failing to pay the mortgage on their property for a certain length of time (usually 6-12 months or longer). The bank that made the mortgage loan takes the home into their possession and then sells it for a discount.

I worked with a realtor to find this property, which was in a good neighborhood, was in solid condition, and with just a little elbow grease could be ready to rent. I then figured out how to make it happen from a financial perspective. My Dad previously told me he wanted to invest in something that generated passive income. I made him a proposal. If he fronted the money for the down payment and we applied for a loan together, I would run the rental and he would benefit from gaining equity and a little monthly income.

We've owned this duplex for the past ten years, and it now has about $70,000 in equity and makes about $500 every month in rental income.

**Disclaimer:* *Purchasing rental properties is* not *for everyone. They require a certain amount of upkeep, general maintenance work, and take more time than the other two types of income listed. Certain pitfalls and additional risks are associated with owning rental properties. As an example, poor tenant choices or an un-rented unit can add unplanned monthly expenses. As such, it's best to have two to four months of cash reserves in addition to down payment money before investing. As a student, you'll want a great mentor who is already a property investor to walk you through the ins and outs of rental property ownership.*

EXPENSES AND BUDGETING

Benjamin Franklin is quoted as saying: *"Beware of little expenses; a small leak will sink a great ship."* In the previous chapter, you learned about the various kinds of income. In this chapter, you'll learn about the expenses that go along with living a normal life. These two points are critical to know because they make up what will become **your budget—the inflow and outflow of money on a monthly basis.** I've counseled thousands of individuals, couples, and students, and those who were financially astute worked from a budget. Those who were debt disasters did not.

Before diving into budgeting, let's first go through the kinds of expenses you'll include in your budget. There are two categories: fixed expenses and variable expenses.

Fixed expenses are bills that remain the same month after month. The amounts of these bills are agreed upon, usually because of a contracted program (like a monthly gym membership) or because you're paying for something over a period of time (like a car or a home). The fixed expenses list can be as long or as short as you make it. It all depends on how many fixed expenses you have committed to on a monthly basis.

The following list of payments could all be included in a fixed monthly expense column:

- Mortgage or Rent
- Car Payment
- Other Car-Related Expenses (Insurance, Registration, Periodic Maintenance, etc.)
- Cable
- Student Loan
- Gym Membership
- Child Care
- Cell Phone
- Netflix

Variable expenses are bills, payments, and expenditures that will vary from month to month. While some of these can be larger, many variable expenses are in the $5 to $10 range; as Benjamin Franklin said, even these small costs can "sink great ships."

A budget becomes essential for most people because while they can manage their fixed expenses, they have no handle on what their variable expenses truly are. They end up spending more than they make in a month, having more month at the end of their money.

The following list could be included in the monthly variable expense column:

- Groceries
- Dining out
- Entertainment
- Travel
- Gifts
- Car maintenance
- Hair care / salon
- Clothes & shoes
- In-app purchases

In my book *30 Days To $1K*, I suggest getting a small pocket-sized spiral-bound notebook to carry with you for a couple of weeks. You can also track your spending on your phone with an app called Pocket Expense, but writing down what you spend makes the numbers more real. Studies have found that the mere act of writing information down causes different parts of your brain to fire.[1] Because the majority of payments made today are digital, it's easy to forget what you bought or how much you spent in a day. After all, breaking a $20, $50, or $100 bill is harder to do than swiping a debit card. When you record the $4.50 you spent on energy drinks or coffee twice in one week, it may cause you to stop and think before doing it again, or at least opt for the $2 version!

Record *everything* you spend money on for the next

two weeks to see which categories you need to add to your variable expenses budget. While many of the expenses will come as no surprise, you'll no doubt wonder about a few of them and ponder how much you've spent through the years.

Budgeting

Budgeting, or creating a budget, may have a negative connotation for some people because it sounds so restrictive. Most people imagine having to cut back on what makes you happy (like buying shoes, video games, or going to the movies). The main reason to create a budget is to allow for MORE freedom, flexibility, and choice in your life, not less. In reality, those who operate with no budget aren't spending money on their highest goals and aspirations—they're dropping money regularly and carelessly on things that might not be considered a high priority. Then, when it comes to high priority items or activities, they might not be able to afford them.

For example, a friend of mine named Amanda recently graduated from college and has an intense desire to travel the world. She went on a study abroad trip in college to Europe and became instantly hooked on the backpacker lifestyle. However, after graduation, she got an apartment, bought a car, realized how much she'd borrowed in student loans, and ate out every day for lunch (and sometimes dinner). When I met her for lunch one day, she told me how down she was about her situation—she never had money. She felt like her travel dreams were getting further away, and she wasn't happy.

When I asked her if she was sticking to her budget, she asked, "What budget?"

"That's part of your solution," I told her. I pulled out a budgeting form and we got to work putting together her fixed and variable expenses. We looked at her overall income on a monthly basis and wrote down her big picture goals. Her driving goals were traveling the world, paying off debt, and having a family, in that order. At this point, things started to click for her.

Amanda's rough estimated budget looked like this:

Monthly Take Home Pay	$2563		
Other Income			
Fixed Expenses		**Variable Expenses**	
Rent:	$600	Gas:	$80
Car Payment:	$275	Groceries:	$250
Student Loans:	$350	Clothing:	$100
Cell Phone:	$100	Entertainment:	$200
Gym:	$75	Credit Card:	$200
Internet:	$50	Utilities:	$80
Other:		Hair Care:	$50
Other:		Dining Out:	$300
Other:		Gifts:	
Total Income	$2563		
Total Expenses	$2710		
Total	-147		

"I'm spending way too much on eating out, aren't I?"

"That depends on whether it's a high priority for you. Given your current list of goals and the limited amount of extra money you have for a travel fund, I'd say yes, you are spending too much on eating out. And, if travel is *really* a priority, you might even consider making other adjustments to your budget. Do you see any other areas to cut back?"

After chewing on the end of her pen for bit, Amanda said, "My parents have offered to let me move home for a while. I'm not super excited by that idea, but it would allow me to put money away for a trip."

"And, you wouldn't be tied down by an apartment lease," I offered. "Anything else?"

"I got wrapped up in this new gym close to the apartment because it's super fancy and the amenities are ridiculous. The only problem is that it's $75 a month."

"Does it get you closer to or farther away from your goals?" I asked.

"I still want to work out, but fancy locker rooms aren't getting me closer to Europe," she said.

"Anything else?" I asked, digging for more realizations.

"Well, my student loans eat up a big chunk of my take-home pay. I can't do anything about that now, but I sure wish I'd applied for more scholarships or not borrowed as much," she said.

I suggested asking about student loan repayment benefits through her employer or finding grants specifically for debt forgiveness.

At the end of our hour-long budgeting jam session, I

asked Amanda how she was feeling about what we did and what steps she would take to create positive momentum toward her goals. Her reply was typical for those I've helped through the budgeting process.

"I actually feel really liberated. What felt like a jail cell was a prison of my own making. I felt like my finances were dictating my life, and now I know that I get to dictate my life through my finances, my choices, and my spending. It's time to make changes. For starters, I'm going to move home and ditch the gym membership for at least the next 12 months."

Setting The Budgeting Habit

While your income may be small right now as a student, and your expenses limited to more wants than needs (because your parents cover most of that), **setting the habit of budgeting now is crucial to your success once you're finished with school and out on your own.**

To illustrate why developing a budgeting habit is crucial, let's do a quick review from Part One:

In Chapter One, you learned that you are expensive. When you set a budget and know how much is coming in and going out, you'll realize how big some of those expenses are and A) appreciate your parents for picking up the tab, and B) save up for those expenses in the future, knowing you can't afford them on your own right now.

In Chapter Two, you learned that your financial success in life is entirely up to you, and your parents don't want to support you forever. Show me someone who has great financial success in life and I guarantee you they've been a budgeter for a long time. It's said that the difference between millionaires and billionaires is the billionaires know where every nickel is spent. In other words, they know their budgets inside and out!

In Chapter Three, you learned that when expenses exceed income, that's bad! There are two ways to know if your expenses have exceeded your income—either you're broke (or in debt) or you've kept track of everything you've made and spent over the course of a month. Your budget is the key to having more money at the end of the month.

In Chapter Four, you learned that your friends and family influence your money values. While the budget won't necessarily shield you from hearing bits of "money wisdom" dropped from time to time, you can prove your friends wrong when they say, "It's just so hard to save money," by setting the budgeting habit early.

Setting the habit is simple—make the first Saturday of every month the day when you put together all of your anticipated income and your anticipated expenses in your budgeting form. Use that small notebook or the Pocket Expense app you used to record your expenses as your guide. Even if the budget rarely changes, taking time each month to put this habit into practice will propel you into another money stratosphere by your early 20s. Using software can make this entire process easier as well. Consider using apps like Mint.com, Yodlee.com, or YNAB.com to streamline the way you gather this information every week or month.

You can find sample budgeting sheets as well as software and application reviews at **www.MoneySavvy.com/Budgets**

REMEMBER: **It's far better to have more money at the end of your month than more month at the end of your money.**

The Family Budget

One of the most eye-opening experiences for both me and my kids was showing them our family budget. Since none of them are old enough to be working part-time and the only "income" they receive is an allowance, our family income looked like a lot of money to them. However, once they saw where that money went on a monthly basis, they were far more inquisitive about what things cost, they were more grateful for new clothes and shoes, AND they pitched in more to "earn their fair share."

Take your household as an example. Do you have any idea how much the utility bills are? Do you know how much your family spends on groceries each week or month? How about the athletics, clubs, or other activities you may be involved in…any idea what those cost a month?

In most schools today, financial education is barely addressed, and most high school seniors still have no idea how much it costs to run a household. Unfortunately, we don't figure that out until we're in our first home, surprised by the monthly costs.

While some parents are less likely to share their income

than I am with my kids, asking about expenses around the house can be very eye-opening. Ask your parents what it costs to run your home—what they pay for your car insurance alone may blow you away. In the process of having this discussion with them, they may realize the need for a more formal family budget!

I believe family budgeting should happen in every house in America. After all, *everyone* in the house plays a part in what it costs to operate the place. Shouldn't *everyone* be in the know? If you're willing to broach the topic with your parents, start by asking for the sake of planning out your future. They may be pleasantly surprised you asked!

SAVING AND INVESTING

The primary reason to create a budget is so you set aside money to save and invest prior to spending it all each month. Much like getting in the habit of keeping a budget, you also need to get in the habit of putting money away each month in a savings account and/or investments. (Are you picking up the fact that there are specific Money Savvy Habits that lead to financial success?)

The habit of saving and investing is the one surefire habit that will help you achieve financial independence—that point in your life when you don't have to work for anyone. Whether that's retirement, working for yourself, or managing and living off of your rental or dividend income, the ONLY way this will happen is if you develop and continue the savings habit. Back in Chapter Three, I mentioned a book called *The Richest Man In Babylon* by Richard S. Clason. The richest man became that way by following the rule of

10%: 10% of what he made was his to keep.

What Am I Saving For?

From the time my kids were old enough to understand money, we talked to them about having an emergency fund. Whenever they received money from family for their birthdays and other holidays, a large chunk of it went to their emergency savings accounts. I set savings goals they had to hit before any of the money could be taken out and used. By the age of five, they had to have at least $300. By the age of seven, $400. And by the time they were nine they had to have saved $500 in emergency savings. As of the time of this writing, my eight year-old has over $1,000 in his emergency fund!

"What kind of emergency is an eight year-old going to have?" Is the question I get when I tell this story at events. My answer is always the same—I hope they don't have any emergencies until they're at least a teenager. But if they have an emergency fund at five, they'll have one at 15, and 25, and 35, and 45…catch my drift?

At one point my middle son asked me, "Dad, what am I saving for?" If you're at all like him you might be asking the same question. The answer is that you're saving for three things:

1. To build an emergency fund

2. For short-term purchases

3. For long-term purchases

The emergency fund is critical for a number of reasons, and if you don't have at least a few hundred dollars in emergency money right now, that is where you should begin. As I mentioned, the logic behind having my kids save for emergencies is about setting the right habits while they're young and impressionable. Ideally, if something should happen in their lives that requires they have money set aside for an emergency, they'll have it (and then some). These emergencies are things like car repairs, health challenges, home or apartment repairs, and anything else that comes out of nowhere.

The other reason for having a healthy emergency fund is that a predicting factor of whether a student will finish college is having at least $500 in an emergency savings account. When a student gets down to the last $50 or less in their account and has bills coming due, it's stressful. Faced with taking the necessary actions to cover the bills (borrowing, working more hours, going without in other areas) or dropping out, many students will drop out because it seems like the safer option. You'd be amazed at the number of students who don't have *any* amount of emergency savings when they enroll in college.

Interestingly, our kids did the same thing my wife and I had done years before as we became more aggressive about saving and investing. The more money that accumulated in their accounts, the more they wanted to contribute to them. They all get super excited about seeing that number grow week after week, month after month.

The opposite mentality is the case when someone has

any amount of credit card debt. The logic typically used here is, "I want this flat panel TV but I can't pay cash for it. Oh well, what's another $500 on my credit card? I already owe $3,000." **Saving tends to create more savings and debt tends to create more debt!**

A good rule of thumb is to have $500 to $1,000 in an emergency savings account. This could be held in either a money market account or a savings account that is NOT easily accessible with an ATM card. Money Market Accounts are very similar to savings accounts but offer a slightly higher interest rate on savings.

Short-term purchases for students could be things like a new phone, athletic equipment for next season, spring break trips with friends, or anything else that you may buy in the next 0-18 months. Obviously, you must develop the ability to look ahead and plan for some of your purchases as a Money Savvy Student. The trap that ensnares most students is the desire for instant gratification. The magic bullet that makes all of this easier has already been covered—budget your money and you'll always have it!

Long-term purchases include things like buying a car, saving money for college, a down payment on a future property, traveling abroad, or buying a new laptop. The amount of the purchase isn't what makes it a long-term item; it's the fact that you're looking far enough ahead to predict what might be needed down the road. If your parents have ever had to replace their roof, their furnace, or had a major auto repair, they know all about long-term savings. Some of the most expensive things that happen in our lives are very predictable, yet the majority of people have no short- or long-term savings…probably because their expenses are greater than their income!

When Should I Start Investing?

After speaking at a college event, a student came to me and asked what they should do with the $2,000 they had saved up. I talked about investing and they wanted to know where to put the money to get the greatest return on their investment. Essentially, they were asking me what stock or mutual fund they should buy to make the most of their money.

My response wasn't what they were hoping for, as I asked them how much they had in an emergency fund and what kinds of purchases they anticipated making in the next 18 months. He hinted at possibly needing a new laptop in the next year or so because his was slowing down. Other than that, he didn't foresee any major purchases. I suggested he put the $2,000 away, separating it into a couple of buckets—$1,000 for emergencies, and $1,000 for short- and long-term savings.

"What about investing the money?" came the reply.

"What I hear in your question is how do you invest the money to make the most in return. The key right now based on the amount of money you have is investor behavior, not investor performance. Investor performance is like asking, "How much can I make?" Investor behavior is committing to a certain amount invested every month, year after year. To be very blunt, without in-depth knowledge, you'd have to take a pretty big risk in the stock market to make a significant return on your $2,000. What I'd rather you do is set yourself up for financial success, protect yourself from emergencies, and then decide to put $25 to $100 a month in a stock or mutual fund while you're in college. That habit, once set, is great investor behavior."

That student emailed me about a week later telling me he did, in fact, put $1,000 away in a money market account for emergencies and put the other $1,000 in a "computer fund" he started on SmartyPig.com. He said his goal was to begin putting $50 a month in long-term investments and to work on his investor behavior!

The $16,000 Millionaire - Using the Power of Compounding

People frequently ask me, "When should I start investing?" The answer is NOW. Want to become a millionaire by the time you're 65? It will only cost you $16,000. $4,000 invested for four years in a row, allowed to compound at 10% annually, will grow to over $1,000,000 if never touched again.

The chart on the next page shows how the $4,000 annual investment grows when earning a 10% annual return compounded on itself.

The $16,000 Millionaire - Using the Power of Compounding

Interest Rate = 10%

*Note: This chart assumes annual compounding

Year	Annual Investment	Balance	Interest	Ending Balance
1	$4,000	$4,000	$400	$4,400
2	$4,000	$8,400	$840	$9,240
3	$4,000	$13,240	$1,324	$14,564
4	$4,000	$18,564	$1,856	$20,420
5		$20,420	$2,042	$22,462
6		$22,462	$2,246	$24,709
7		$24,709	$2,471	$27,180
8		$27,180	$2,718	$29,898
9		$29,898	$2,990	$32,887
10		$32,887	$3,289	$36,176
11		$36,176	$3,618	$39,794
12		$39,794	$3,979	$43,773
13		$43,773	$4,377	$48,150
14		$48,150	$4,815	$52,965
15		$52,965	$5,297	$58,262
16		$58,262	$5,826	$64,088
17		$64,088	$6,409	$70,497
18		$70,497	$7,050	$77,546
19		$77,546	$7,755	$85,301
20		$85,301	$8,530	$93,831
21		$93,831	$9,383	$103,214
22		$103,214	$10,321	$113,536
23		$113,536	$11,354	$124,889
24		$124,889	$12,489	$137,378
25		$137,378	$13,738	$151,116
26		$151,116	$15,112	$166,228
27		$166,228	$16,623	$182,850
28		$182,850	$18,285	$201,135
29		$201,135	$20,114	$221,249
30		$221,249	$22,125	$243,374
31		$243,374	$24,337	$267,711
32		$267,711	$26,771	$294,482
33		$294,482	$29,448	$323,931
34		$323,931	$32,393	$356,324
35		$356,324	$35,632	$391,956
36		$391,956	$39,196	$431,152
37		$431,152	$43,115	$474,267
38		$474,267	$47,427	$521,694
39		$521,694	$52,169	$573,863
40		$573,863	$57,386	$631,249
41		$631,249	$63,125	$694,374
42		$694,374	$69,437	$763,812
43		$763,812	$76,381	$840,193
44		$840,193	$84,019	$924,212
45		$924,212	$92,421	*$1,016,633*
46		$1,016,633	$101,663	$1,118,297
47		$1,118,297	$111,830	$1,230,126
48		$1,230,126	$123,013	$1,353,139
49		$1,353,139	$135,314	$1,488,453
50		$1,488,453	$148,845	$1,637,298

Compounding happens when the interest you earn on your principal (the initial investment) is added to the balance so that the added interest also earns interest from then on. There are two key ingredients for compound interest to work well in your favor: time and money. When you don't have a lot of money to invest (like when you're young), you have the advantage of having A LOT of time.

In the example above, we are assuming that you could make a 10% annual return year after year, which is not really how the stock market works. Some years you might earn more, some less (you might even lose money some years, depending on your investments). The key here is to start at a young age so the power of compounding interest is unleashed for future growth.

There are two main challenges that Money Savvy Students have to overcome to unleash the power of compounding interest in their lives. The first is understanding the benefits of (and practicing) delayed gratification. Delayed gratification is the ability to put off something that is fun or rewarding now for the greater benefit of something fun or pleasurable later. Using the $4,000 a year example from above, think for a moment what you could do with $4,000 every year for four years. What comes to mind?

- New clothes
- New shoes
- A vacation
- A car
- Tickets to professional athletic events
- Donating the money to charity

Without a doubt you could find *something* to do with the money that would add to your life. Practicing delayed gratification means knowing you could have a lot of fun with that money, but choosing instead to do something with the money for a greater (and later) good.

The second main challenge to overcome is setting (and sticking to) the habit of routinely putting money away for future growth. This becomes easier once you have your emergency fund established, your savings goals and strategies in place, and a set amount directed toward compound growth. If $4,000 seems way too unattainable, even putting $25 a month in investment accounts will begin the process needed to turbocharge your compounding interest.

Where Should I Invest?

There is no easy answer to the question, "Where should I invest?" In all reality, every single person could have their own customized investment plan depending on their goals, dreams, income, and family circumstances. However, this book isn't meant to give you a deep understanding of every level of investing. The goal IS to give you enough information to inspire you to learn more about what you can do with the money you'll accumulate. To get you started on this path, here are the "buckets" you can put money in right now:

ROTH IRA: Named after the late Senator William Roth, this Individual Retirement Account allows you to invest up to a certain amount of money per year in stocks, bonds, and mutual funds. The money invested is after-tax dollars, meaning you've paid income tax on that money before investing. The power of the ROTH IRA is in the fact that the interest earned on those investments grows tax-free for the rest of your life. One reason this is so powerful for you is that your tax rate is lower today than it will be when you're much older and making more money.

401(k): The 401(k) is a retirement vehicle usually offered by your employer. Most companies today allow you to contribute money from your paycheck into the company 401(k) plan. Depending on the employer, they may offer to match your contributions to the 401(k) up to a certain amount of your salary. As an example, your company might match your investment dollar-for-dollar up to 6% of your salary. The investment into a 401(k) plan is made with pre-tax dollars, meaning the money you put in has not been calculated into your taxable income. By lowering your taxable income, the amount you pay in taxes is also lower. With the right investments, your 401(k) will grow throughout your life. However, when it comes time to withdraw the money at retirement, you'll pay taxes on the growth.

Brokerage Account: While the ROTH IRA and the 401(k) are considered to be retirement vehicles, a brokerage account is a different kind of bucket. The brokerage account allows you to transfer money in and out when convenient or needed, where retirement buckets will charge a fee and a penalty for withdrawing early. Brokerage accounts can be opened by someone of any age, though anyone under the age of 18 will have to have a custodian for the account – usually a parent or guardian. The brokerage account allows you to invest in the same stocks, bonds, and mutual funds you would in your ROTH IRA or 401(k). The biggest difference is that the money invested is after-tax money, and only the growth of your funds is subject to taxes.

The above accounts are referred to as "buckets." The difference between the different varieties of buckets is based on how that money is taxed. Two are listed as retirement buckets, while one is not. The retirement buckets give tax incentives for investing money for the long haul in an attempt to reward us for planning for retirement.

The money put into each bucket can either be stored as "cash" or moved into various investments: stocks, bonds, mutual funds, and other more complicated investment vehicles.

What's In The Buckets?

Stocks. These refer to **shares of companies** that are sold to investors who wish to own part of the overall value of the business – the assets and earnings.

Bonds. Bonds are different from stocks in that a bond is a **debt instrument**, while stocks are a piece of ownership. When a company issues a bond, they're raising money which they will later owe the bondholders, paid out over a certain length of time. In effect, you're loaning money to a company when you buy a bond and they are obligated to pay it back.

Mutual Funds. Mutual Funds can be a **combination of the two**. The mutual fund company takes the funds and invests in stocks and bonds (and sometimes other mutual funds). While mutual funds are considered a less risky investment because the money is distributed over a variety of investments, there is also a management fee associated with a company managing those funds. There are more mutual funds offered than there are individual stocks and bonds in existence!

REITs. REITs, or Real Estate Investment Trusts, **invest in land or real estate** and will generally pay a monthly, quarterly, or annual dividend. By owning a REIT, you are sharing in the ownership of a property with other investors.

The Quick-Start Checklist:

While the sheer amount of information surrounding saving and investing can be overwhelming, don't let that stop you from taking action. The key is to get started. The tremendous opportunity you have on your side is TIME. By forming a saving and investing habit early, even small and seemingly insignificant amounts invested can grow exponentially over time.

To get you started quickly, do the following:

1. Set-up a savings account with a goal of having at least $500 in it continuously. I recommend SmartyPig.com, though you can easily set this up through your local bank or credit union. (You may already have a savings account, though it's probably more of a "put and take" account. Put a little in, take a little out...) Get to the $500 mark as soon as possible, then turn your focus towards long-term saving and investing.

2. Open a ROTH IRA account through a company like Vanguard.com. Vanguard has lower fees than most other investment firms when it comes to beginners. You can put up to $5,500 a year in your ROTH IRA (based on 2016 guidelines).

3. Expand your knowledge. If the notion of investing money in the various vehicles above is interesting to you, do your research. There are a variety of educational websites and resources you can use to expand your knowledge of investing. Find a detailed listing of these here: www.MoneySavvy.com/Invest.

CREDIT AND BORROWING

Your Credit Score

Nothing has had a more profound impact on the economic world around us than credit and borrowing in the way of mortgages, credit cards, and car loans. While you may or may not have a car loan or credit card yet, it's important to know the key piece of information used by banks and credit unions to determine if you're creditworthy: your credit score.

Every person with a social security number has a credit score tied to their name. There are three Credit Reporting Agencies (CRAs) that collect payment, balance data from creditors, and issue the credit score. These three CRAs are Experian, Equifax, and TransUnion.

If a young person has never had a loan in their name, their score would show up as a zero or a No Score, whereas someone who has already applied for and maintained some level of debt and related payments would have a score between 300 and 850. **Your credit score is an indicator of how responsible you've been with loans, credit cards, and other items tied to your credit history (like utility bills, phone bills, etc.).** Low scores (in the 300-600 range) are indicative of someone who doesn't pay their bills on time, has missed payments, or has let loans go into default (stopped paying). Higher scores (in the 600-850 range) are indicative of someone who has a mix of various debt instruments (like a car loan and a credit card) and has made payments on time every month since the loans began.

This number will determine how expensive or cheap it is for you to borrow money later in life, which is crucial for you to understand. The lower your credit score, the higher the interest rates on your loans, which makes them more expensive in the long run. Conversely, the higher your credit score, the lower the interest rates on your loans, which makes them cheaper in the long run.

If you were shopping for a car and it was time to line up the financing for the vehicle, the dealership would pull your credit score to determine your loan interest rate. The score pulled is a snapshot in time of what your credit looks like on that day. If your credit was pulled a few weeks from now, the score might move up or down depending on the financial transactions you made during that time. Your credit score is comprised of the following:

35% Payment History: Your payment history is the record of on-time payments you've made over the life of a loan or credit card history. The "cleaner" your payment history (meaning more on-time payments), the higher your score tends to be. It's essential to your credit score that you make all of your payments on time or before they're due.

30% Amounts Owed: Creditors that will potentially lend you money want to know how much you have borrowed already and the amount of your current balance as compared to what you originally borrowed. This gives them a sense of your utilization percentage. When a high percentage of your available credit has been used, it can mean you may be overextended on credit. In other words, you have used all or almost all of your available credit.

15% Length of Credit History: The length of your credit history takes into account how long you've had active accounts reporting to your credit report. As a young person, this is where your score may suffer. If you're going after your first loan, you are only now establishing credit and the length of your credit history will be very short.

10% Credit Mix: Your score is based (albeit a small amount) on the mix of accounts that show up on your credit report. A higher score will have installment loans (like car loans), revolving accounts (credit cards), and a mortgage (home loan). As a student, your best bet for a higher score is to have a credit card for emergencies, and potentially an installment loan (like an auto loan or a 'credit-builder loan' available at most credit unions). It's a good idea to apply for a credit card, a credit-builder loan, or an installment loan while in your teens or early 20s to begin building your credit history.

10% New Credit: Another minor consideration in factoring your credit score is the amount of new credit you've applied for in the recent past. This portion of the score looks at the accounts you've opened in the last 30-90 days. Multiple new accounts opened in a short amount of time can be negative as it gives you the opportunity to overextend yourself. Several new accounts opened in a short amount of time will lower your score.

It may be a few years before your credit score becomes important. Whether you know your credit score or not, it is constantly tracked by the Credit Reporting Agencies; any and all missteps when it comes to borrowing will end up affecting your score. When you're ready to buy a car, get into an apartment of your own, take out a loan on a home, or even apply for your first full-time job, your credit score will usually be taken into consideration.

It's reported that a vast majority of credit reports have faulty or erroneous information reported to them, causing consumer credit scores to be artificially low. In 2003, the Federal Trade Commission enacted the Fair Credit Reporting Act, which protects consumers in a variety of ways. It's important to know your rights when it comes to pulling and verifying the data that shows up on your credit report. Here's how you're protected:

1. The data reported to the Credit Reporting Agencies MUST be true and validated. If for any reason you think activity was reported to your credit report in error, you can request the CRAs verify the information or have it removed within 30 days.

2. You can request one copy of your credit report from each of the CRAs every year. It's best to space them out about every four months so you keep track of events throughout the year. The website to request your free copy: www.annualcreditreport.com.

By keeping tabs on your credit report and corresponding score, you'll save yourself MASSIVE amounts of money over the life of your loans, mortgages, and credit cards. A Money Savvy Habit of checking your score regularly should start before you need the credit!

Borrowing - Credit Cards and Loans

Credit Cards

Credit cards are a very pervasive part of life today. After all, I just recommended that getting a credit card can be a great way to begin building credit history. While credit cards create remarkable convenience when paying for everyday items, that convenience does come with a price if the card isn't managed properly. This section will give you a greater understanding of how people can become stuck in credit card debt due to fees, interest rates, and a general misunderstanding of how payments are applied.

The majority of credit cards today have interest rates somewhere in the 12%–24% range. These rates are significantly higher than what you'd see on a car loan because they are considered an "unsecured loan." An unsecured loan is money lent to a borrower on something intangible or difficult to repossess. Credit cards are used to purchase everything from gas and groceries to clothing and travel. These things are hard to swing by and pick up should you stop paying your bills. To protect themselves from loss, lending institutions will give you a credit card with a high interest rate. Because it's a higher risk for the lender, they charge a higher rate to borrow the funds.

Credit cards are both useful and dangerous to your financial well-being if not used properly. Not only are the interest rates higher than most other financial instruments, credit card companies make it ridiculously easy to pay only the minimum on your account on a monthly basis. For most credit card companies, the minimum amount due is equal to around 2% of your outstanding balance. That means if you've put $3,000 on your credit card, the credit card company will require that you pay at least $60 per month as your minimum payment. What they may not make clear is that when the interest is factored in, your minimum payment may barely cover the interest charged. If your credit card interest rate is 19.9%, here are how the numbers break down:

$3,000 Balance

x19.9% Interest

= $597 in annual interest

÷12 months

= $49.75 per month in interest

Walking you through the above example, your $3,000 balance is charged an *annual percentage rate* (or APR) of 19.9%. For the year, your interest charges would amount to $597. If you divide $597 by 12 months (because we want to figure this month's interest expense), you come up with $49.75 in interest. Now, remember, your minimum payment on this credit card is $60 a month.

If you thought that $60 payment was going straight to the amount owed, think again. Only $11.25 of your $60.00 is applied to the principal balance. Assuming you didn't charge anything else to your credit card, next month your $60 payment will break down to $11.44 going to principal and $49.56 to interest. In two months, you sent $120 to your credit card company, but only $22.69 went toward the total amount owed.

If you're wondering how long it will take you to pay off $3,000 in credit card debt at 19.9% interest with payments of $60 a month, the answer is 108 months. That's nine years of making minimum payments. Your total interest expense would be $3,454. The total you end up paying is DOUBLE your original debt amount, plus $454.

This is how people get into serious problems with credit

card debt. They send in payment after payment, yet never make any forward progress on knocking out their debt. The one foolproof way to avoid falling into this trap is to remember that credit cards are useful tools when traveling or if you have an absolute emergency, but otherwise they should stay at home. This is the mantra I've taught students for years: "If I can eat it, drink it, or wear it, it doesn't go on plastic!"

Say it out loud with me:

"If I can eat it, drink it, or wear it, it doesn't go on plastic!"

You're so Savvy.

Loans

While it may seem like everyone borrows money today, most people don't have the foggiest clue about an important aspect of borrowing: what that money *actually* costs.

Borrowing money in large amounts means taking out a loan from a bank or credit union. A large amount borrowed from the financial institution of your choosing will carry with it an interest rate which varies depending on your credit score. As of the time of this writing, someone with a high credit score can get a car loan for a low interest rate of 1.99%. That's considered ridiculously cheap money. On the opposite side of the spectrum, someone with a low credit score may be charged upwards of 15%-20% for the same car and the same loan.

If you weren't a Money Savvy Student, you'd go into a car dealership not caring about the interest rate; you'd just want the car! Since you are a Money Savvy Student, you know there are more factors to consider when picking out your sweet ride—like how much will that loan *actually* cost in the long run?

Let's assume that Mike is not so Savvy. Mike has a low credit score because he got a credit card at a department store when he turned 18 and forgot to make the payments on it. It's since been turned over to a collections agency. As a result, the payment history is not positive on his credit report, resulting in a very low score.

Mike wants a $15,000 car badly and is willing to do anything to get it. The car dealership knows this and offers a seven-year car loan at 18% interest.

Amount Financed	Interest Rate	Payment	Terms	Total
$15,000	18%	$315	84 mos.	$26,482

As you can see from the numbers above, the $15,000 car will end up costing well over $26,000 by the time the interest is factored in. Surely, Molly will have a different approach.

Money Savvy Molly doesn't have much of a credit history, but after working with her local banker or credit union loan officer, she was approved for a car loan for the same $15,000 car with a 3.9% interest rate. She decided on a five-year loan to keep the payments relatively low, and she knows she can send in extra payments when she has the funds. Her situation looks like this:

Amount Financed	Interest Rate	Payment	Terms	Total
$15,000	3.9%	$276	60 mos.	$16,534

In case you were looking for reasons to pay closer attention to the interest rate charged on your loans, the above example gives you about 10,000 of them. The difference between Mike's loan and Molly's loan is $10,000 AND two full years of payments! Mike has a loan term of 84 months and a HIGHER payment than Molly, who will pay nearly $40 less a month for only 60 months.

The one major difference between Mike and Molly was that Mike was careless about the credit card debt he acquired at the mall. A insignificant balance overlooked can cause a MAJOR expense down the road. **Being Money Savvy is about making sound decisions with the debt you have and being in the know when you're securing other loans, whether for a vehicle, for college, or for a home.**

DEBT

Americans LOVE debt. Many would say they hate it and love it at the same time. Debt is an incredibly helpful tool that allows people to buy homes, cars, televisions, and furniture they otherwise might not be able to purchase right now. However, there are limits that should be understood when it comes to taking on debt. Those limits are being pushed to the edges of viability in today's economy.

As of the time of this printing, the amounts of debt outstanding in America in various forms are as follows:[1]

- Mortgage Debt: $13.9 Trillion

- Student Loan Debt $1.35 Trillion

- Automobile Debt: $1.1 Trillion

- Credit Card Debt: $947 Billion

While some debt is useful, too much of it is seriously

problematic. For those who are not Savvy when it comes to handling their finances (debt payments, spending, budgeting, saving, etc.), the fact that there is always someone willing to give you more of it compounds the problem. If you're in debt way over your head, I guarantee you there is someone willing to give you even more at a higher interest rate. There is often an assumption that, "No one would give it to me if I couldn't afford it." It's simply not true. There is ALWAYS someone who will extend you credit and allow you to go deeper in debt. In fact, some companies specifically prey on people who don't have a clue.

As a student, you'll soon be faced with opportunities to go into debt—namely through student loans and credit cards. While the perils of student loan debt are covered more in Section Three, let me point out the fact that student loan debt is the second highest debt balance next to home mortgages in the U.S. According to the Congressional Budget Office, over 25% of these loans are in default, meaning the people who've acquired the debt are no longer making payments.[2]

After having presented on over 700 campuses, one common theme was the fact that most students had no idea how much they'd borrowed and no concept of how much their future payments would be. It's easy to see how the lack of understanding regarding how loans work could lead to a situation where one in every four loans is not being paid back.

I created a documentary that highlights the causes and repercussions of student debt that is now being used in high schools and colleges across the country. *Broke, Busted, & Disgusted* helps students understand the dangers of borrowing without thinking about the ramifications. The website www.BrokeBustedDisgusted.com has links to the film and a discussion guide students can use to become more aware of the ways to minimize borrowing.

While student debt grows exponentially, the amount of credit card debt taken on by students has also increased dramatically. Though credit card companies can no longer set up tables on campus and sign students up for a credit card in exchange for a frisbee, t-shirt, or one pound bag of M&M's, what they can still do is mail you credit card applications. Pay close attention to your mailbox as a student to see how many credit applications you receive. While the applications may seem innocent, credit card companies know that if you apply for a card in college (or before), you'll hold that card for up to 8 years, making them massive profits along the way!

If you're wondering how you can be approved for a credit card before ever having a full-time job or significant income, you're not alone. I asked a credit card representative who happened to be on campus some years ago how they got away with giving out credit cards to students with no verifiable income. Her response was not what I expected. She said with every application that's filled out by a student, there is an assumed co-signer on that card from the card issuing company's perspective. In other words, they assume that if you get in a bind financially, your parents will more than likely bail you out.

Because the use of debt in our society is so prevalent, the bottom line when it comes to the handling and understanding of debt is *be informed*. Chapter Eight high-lighted the need to understand your credit score, how interest rate impacts the overall cost of your debt, and how payments are applied to credit cards. All of these points are essential to understand.

What you should take from Chapter Nine is that debt is a tool, used differently by everyone. It has the ability to enhance your life in the way of buying your first car or home, investing in your education, or even buying your first set of furniture. However, it also has the ability to make life significantly harder than it needs to be if you overuse it. Before you take on major debt of any kind (over a paycheck's worth), be sure to consult with a mentor of yours who is knowledgeable about the topic and can help guide you to the best decision.

INSURANCE

Look up the definition of insurance and you'll find it is a product typically purchased to protect against financial loss. As a student, the only insurance you're likely concerned about is car insurance (and I'm sure your parents complain loudly about the price of it). There are other kinds of insurance that adults have, which might include: life insurance, homeowners insurance, renters insurance, health insurance, disability insurance, and often an umbrella liability insurance policy that covers someone for a variety of losses or issues. These will all be briefly described in this chapter.

Here's a high-level overview of how insurance companies work. The basis of any insurance business, whether we're talking about life insurance, car insurance, or homeowners insurance, is RISK. Insurance companies charge a monthly premium for the type of insurance you've purchased. The premium ranges from high to low based on the amount of risk the insurance company is agreeing to take on.

If you're a young driver, you're at a higher risk of being in an accident, and insurance companies charge a higher premium for teenagers than they charge someone older than 25. Similarly, if you have received a number of speeding tickets or other moving violations (like running a red light), your premiums will go up. Essentially, the insurance companies keep track of your driving ability, calculate the risk associated with your driving record, and price it accordingly.

Most people don't know that not only do insurance companies keep track of your driving record, but they're also tracking your credit score. Research has shown that your credit score (which measures how responsible you are with your money) is a prime indicator of how responsible you are behind the wheel.

Between the ages of 16 and 25, the cost of insuring you to drive a vehicle is compared to highway robbery. According to a survey done for Nationwide, the cost to insure a teenage driver increases the premium over $800 per year.[1] That is *just* to insure you to drive the car. Remember in Chapter One when you learned that you are expensive? Add this amount to the general expense category of raising a kid.

The auto insurance policy your parents pay for (or maybe you pay for yourself) covers the costs related to fixing the vehicle should you get in an accident. Most auto insurance policies have uninsured and underinsured motorist protection, which means if someone runs a red light and collides with your car—whether they have insurance themselves or not—the damages will be covered by your policy. Uninsured motorists are part of the reason that auto insurance has gone up substantially over the past couple of decades. Auto insurance became mandatory in 1927, and if you're ever pulled over, you'll be asked to show proof of insurance.

Homeowners and renters insurance are similar in that they both cover the property and the contents within your home. While renters insurance is relatively inexpensive, homeowners insurance varies in price and can range from affordable to downright expensive. The risk taken on by the insurance company will be the main factor in determining the expense of the premium. Having a security system, added locks or cameras, being close to a fire hydrant or fire station, the location of your neighborhood, or having lots of equity in your home are all factors in determining the overall risk to the insurance company.

If you've borrowed (taken out a mortgage) to buy a home, the lender will require you have insurance on the property. In the event of a house fire, for example, the insurance will cover the rebuilding of the home up to a certain value, protecting both you AND the bank that loaned you the money. Imagine if you didn't have insurance on your home and it burned down—would you have the money to rebuild the house AND continue paying the mortgage payment? Probably not, so having insurance protects you against financial loss.

Disability insurance protects you from the loss of income should you become unable to work. More often than not, your full-time employer will offer a disability policy which will replace a portion of your income if something renders you unable to work. There are both short-term and long-term disability policies. Short-term disability policies will cover a portion of your income once you run out of paid time off (PTO) and sick leave (usually 9 to 52 weeks), and long-term disability policies will cover your income once you've run out of short-term disability, PTO, and sick leave (usually after 52 weeks).

Health insurance is in place to reduce the costs associated with your health care should you need to see a doctor, have a hospital stay, or need surgery. There is a great deal of controversy around the cost of health care, health insurance, and the coverage most families need or receive. It will no doubt continue to be an issue in the future as the costs associated with quality healthcare continue to rise. Students are generally on their parents' health insurance plan until they are finished with school, and can enjoy continued coverage until the age of 26.

Life insurance only pays out in the event of your death. It's often said that it should be called death insurance because of the way it works. People typically purchase life insurance when they have others to take care of in the event of their death, like children or spouses. Very few students have the need for life insurance. However, your family may use life insurance policies as an investment vehicle, so you may be covered and just not know it. When you're employed full-time, your employer will usually offer life insurance as a benefit of employment.

Finally, **an umbrella policy is essentially extra**

liability insurance should you be involved in a lawsuit that your auto, home, or other insurance doesn't cover. Students don't often hold umbrella policies, but don't be surprised if your parents have an umbrella policy over and above what they have in home and auto insurance.

What you need to know is that insurance is a necessity. The only reason you wouldn't have it on your vehicle, your property, or yourself is because you can afford to self-insure. This means you have plenty of money available to you should you ever cause an accident, have a fire that destroys part or all of your home, or become unable to work. Self-insuring requires a significant amount of money set aside—insurance is a much more cost effective option when you're young.

The reason understanding insurance is important at your age is that it's a life expense that's often overlooked. My recommendation would be to inquire of your parents what kinds of insurance they cover for you and what kinds of costs are associated with those policies. By the time you're in your early 20s, you'll want to pay attention to things like:

- The cost of auto insurance for the vehicle you drive AND the vehicle you have your eye on (the cost of insurance alone may make you think twice about the brand new ride!)

- How much health insurance will cost once you turn 26 and are no longer eligible to be on your parents' plan

- How much a renter's insurance policy costs on a monthly basis

- If your employer offers short-term and long-term disability insurance

TAXES

Have you ever wondered where the money comes from to pay teachers? How about the money it takes to keep the lights on in a school building, to keep the building maintained, and to keep the buses running every day? The easy answer is taxes, which are generally divided up into three categories: federal, state, and local.

Taxes are fees imposed by a government on products, income, activity, sales, or property. The fee (or tax) charged is used to support the management, oversight, or delivery of something beneficial to the individual or society. In this chapter, you'll get a high-level understanding of what taxes are, where you're paying them, and what that money is used for.

According to the National Center for Education Statistics, 93% of education spending is funded through state and local taxes.[1] In most states, the bulk of the tax revenue comes from sales and income taxes paid both by individuals and by corporations. On the local level, the taxes come from property taxes paid by homeowners. This amount is based on a percentage of the value of the home and property and is set by local officials, the school board, or the citizenry.

Local tax revenues are the reason for the major differences among schools and school districts when it comes to their amenities, building upkeep, and other associated costs. The more affluent the neighborhood, the greater the amount of local taxes collected to help support the costs of education in that area. Bigger homes with high values equate to more tax revenue for schools. Conversely, a lower income neighborhood will have property values that wouldn't collect as much in tax revenue to help fund schools. This continues to be the widest gap in society where equal educational opportunities are concerned.

While you won't pay property taxes unless or until you become a homeowner, you are paying taxes on an everyday basis whether you know it or not. Every time you buy something at a store, you pay sales tax, which is levied by the state and goes to cover the cost of running the state government (which also helps fund your school). Every time you fill up your tank, a gas tax is levied against you (rolled into your purchase price) and those funds are used to help maintain the quality of our roads, amongst other things.

Perhaps the largest, and most detested and complained about tax of all, is income tax. This is the amount taken out of your paycheck as a W-2 wage earner or paid in as a 1099 contractor, collected by either the state treasurer or the

Internal Revenue Service (IRS). Paid by individuals and corporations alike, income taxes are generally calculated by taking a percentage of your income up to a certain amount. The chart below shows the 2016 percentages taken out of your paycheck determined by your income.[2]

2016 Taxable Income Brackets and Rates (Estimate)			
Rate	Single Filers	Married Joint	Head of Household
10%	$0 – $9,275	$0 – $18,550	$0 – $13,250
15%	$9,276 – $37,650	$18,550 – $75,300	$13,251 – $50,400
25%	$37,651 – $91,150	$75,301 – $151,900	$50,401 – $130,150
28%	$91,151 – $190,150	$151,901 – $231,450	$130,151 – $210,800
33%	$190,151 – $413,350	$231,451 – $413,350	$210,801 – $413,350
35%	$413,351 – $415,050	$413,351 – $466,950	$413,351 – $441,000
39.6%	$415,051+	$466,951+	$441,001+

A student who is making W-2 income, earning $15,000 a year, would pay 10% income tax up to the $9,275 mark, then 15% from $9,275 to $15,000. As you can see, there is a difference if you are "Married Filing Jointly" or filing as the "Head of Household."

No matter which category you fall into, the highest tax bracket is closing in on 40%. If you were in this tax bracket, that would mean you would work for almost five months out of the year JUST to pay your taxes. The other seven months out of the year, the income is yours to keep. In some states like California—a government in dire need of tax revenue—there are people who work six or seven months out of the year to cover state, federal, and local taxes.

Make no mistake, taxes are an essential part of running our country. Imagine having to pay for the services that police officers, firefighters, and other government-run agencies provide to the public. Without a well-run tax system, in the event of an emergency, you'd hear "911, what's your credit card number?"

My recommendation is that you learn and understand the tax system as best you can. **The two greatest expenses we'll ever have in life are taxes and the interest expense on debt.** The books that helped me get a better grasp on taxes were *The Cashflow Quadrant* by Robert Kiyosaki, and *Tax-Free Wealth* by Tom Wheelwright. Understanding how to minimize your tax burden is a key to growing your wealth and being more Money Savvy!

PART 3
Taking Action

If you're anything like most students, you are sick and tired of getting asked, "What do you want to be when you grow up?" or "What do you want to do with your life?"

Candidly, I understand where the frustration comes from because the real answer is: HOW SHOULD I KNOW? I'VE BARELY HAD ANY REAL-LIFE EXPERIENCES.

Look, you're at a stage of life where people have been grooming you to take the next big step in your academic career. For most people, this means higher education, whether that's a community college, university, apprenticeship, or certificate program. The reality is that you are biologically still a child—the last part of your brain to develop is the prefrontal cortex, the part of your brain that allows you to think critically, to look ahead, to make great judgment calls.

This part of your brain has been called the seat of good

judgment because it can predictively look ahead based on the decisions you make today. It typically develops faster in women than in men; some men don't fully develop their prefrontal cortex until they're 25 or older. If you want a great answer to everyone who asks you THOSE questions, just tell them, "I'll let you know once my prefrontal cortex develops."

In my opinion, there are far too many students taking the plunge into very expensive educational institutions before they've thought about what kind of career they'd like to pursue. At one point in time, you could "find yourself" at college, but today's college costs are far too restrictive to do that. Students who meander their way through school end up borrowing far more than they need to, which limits their future options because of restrictive amounts of debt.

Your education thus far has led you to a point where you're either considering which education/career path to pursue OR you're working toward a job through internships, apprenticeships, the military, etc. I applaud you for your effort and hard work so far; now make sure that you're taking action on what you've learned in *The Money Savvy Student.*

I believe taking action is about learning what fires you up in life, figuring out how to live within your means, and taking the necessary steps to build the Money Savvy Habits that will carry you into prosperity for the rest of your life. Because the next phase of your life is where so many students fall down, Part Three will cover aspects of funding college, how to make money using the information you've already learned, and the next steps to take to put this book into practice!

COLLEGE IS EXPENSIVE

Things Are Different Today Than When Your Parents Went To College

When I started delivering financial education programs at high schools and college campuses 12 years ago, students were taking on about $20K in student loans and there were jobs available once they graduated. Their propensity to pay back those loans in under 10 years was high, and the financial stresses were relatively low.

Over the past 12 years, I've seen the student loan debt numbers escalate dramatically. Today, no matter where I'm presenting, it's not uncommon for me to hear students talk about $60,000, $80,000, sometimes well over $100,000 in student loans. The stress they feel about finishing and figuring out "what they want to do with their lives" is equal to the stress they feel about this enormous debt load they've taken on. Most have buried their heads in the sand about the debt amount so they can focus on getting done with their degree.

While the attainment of a degree is still considered the fastest way to achieve success in our society, the reality is that there are a variety of ways to advance in life beyond high school and pursue higher education affordably. Blindly pursuing a four-year degree without examining all of your options may leave you wishing you could go back in time and get a do-over.

Unfortunately, the current laws provide little protection for a student who has borrowed a significant amount in student loans and stops paying them. The result is seriously damaged credit, high penalties, and high interest on the debt in the long run. "Hiding" from your student loans is impossible. They will <u>always</u> find you.

What I'd like to propose is a different way of both looking at how you pursue higher education and how you fund higher education. From this chapter you'll get a new perspective on how to graduate with less debt.

Why Student Loans Are Called Good Debt (But Not All Should Be)

There is a biological phenomenon known as hormesis. It occurs when something in small amounts has a beneficial effect while the same thing in large quantities would be lethal. Take chemotherapy as an example—small doses of chemo drugs are administered in an attempt to "kill" the cancerous cells in a person's body. If large quantities of chemo drugs were administered, it would no doubt be lethal to someone's system.

The same is true of student loan debt. In moderate amounts, student loans are a good thing. They allow students and families who don't have the money to afford school on their own to pursue the coveted degree. It's known as having a "hormetic effect." After all, a moderate amount of debt helped them achieve something worthwhile. The reason Lyndon B. Johnson signed the Higher Education Act in 1965 was to create a student loan system to help students who wanted to go to college but couldn't afford it.

Student loans become toxic when they're too large to be paid off in a reasonable amount of time, if at all. There are multiple factors at play:

- The major you choose – which may or may not have high earning potential

- The amount of money you'll feasibly make in your career choice

- The interest charged on the money borrowed

- How long you plan on making payments

- How effectively you live within your budget

Hundreds of thousands of students have wandered into a debt corner that will hold them back their entire lives. They took advantage of what seemed like "free money" to cover all of their college costs without looking at their future job prospects, future income, and future payments. As a Money

Savvy Student, your goal should be to thoroughly understand the choices you're making when it comes to borrowing, including the future ramifications of that borrowing.

As a society, we've taken to calling student loans "good debt" because the result of taking out student loans is (or should be) a degree that gives you upward mobility in your job. There are, however, cases where the debt taken on was more than an individual could handle after graduation. The "good debt" will quickly become "bad debt" when the recent graduate stops making payments – usually because they don't understand their options when it comes to paying the loans back, and/or their income isn't enough to cover all of their expenses.

The best rule of thumb is never to borrow more than your first year's anticipated gross earnings (if you don't know your anticipated gross earnings because you haven't decided on a career path, sit tight – we'll address that). For example, if you are pursuing a degree in education and plan on being a teacher, it would be best to borrow only as much as a starting teacher makes in a year. According to the National Education Association, the average starting teacher in America makes $36,141.[1] Therefore, your student loan totals shouldn't be much higher than that number. While it's possible to borrow more than this amount, the challenge will become apparent once you've graduated and the payments take up a large chunk of your take-home pay.

If you plan on studying engineering, an entry-level mechanical engineer position on average makes $62,527.[2] Using the logic above, you could borrow around or below that amount and know that you could cover your payments and afford to live with that salary.

The key is to do your research and know the average pay for someone starting in the field you're interested in pursuing. If it is necessary for you to borrow more than that amount, consider using some of the techniques listed below or choosing another school or major with a cost that makes you comfortable.

Funding College

According to The College Board, the average cost of attending a four-year state university is around $80,000, while the average cost of attending a four-year private college is closer to $178,000.[3] Those numbers may not factor in grants and scholarships you've won to help cover the cost of school, but instead reflect the TOTAL cost if you were to pay the full tuition, room, and board out of pocket. To say the least, it costs A LOT of money. That being said, there are dozens of ways to get your college costs covered or reduced so you don't leave school with mountains of debt that take 20+ years to pay off. Here are a few of the ways to make your life after college easier.

Scholarships. There are college scholarship opportunities available to students as early as 3rd grade and going all the way through to Ph.D. programs. Contrary to popular belief, they're NOT reserved for students with amazing grades or financial needs, not saved for the superstar athletes or the physically impaired. If you have a 2.0 and love to skateboard, there's a scholarship application waiting for you. If one of your parents is a firefighter, EMT, or police officer, there's an application waiting for you. I've seen students win awards for being left-handed, for being adopted, for having migraines, and for making the most amazing peanut butter and jelly sandwich. There is a scholarship for nearly everything out there.

Here's the catch: you will NEVER win a scholarship if you don't apply. You may not win the first five or ten applications you fill out, but you may win the 11th through the 15th, and that might be enough to cover your college costs. At the very least, there are awards that will help you cover books and other fees every semester, and it may be as simple as writing a 200-300 word essay.

The key is applying for as many awards as possible. The more you apply, the better you get. The better you get at filling out applications and writing essays, the more scholarship money you may get to cover your college costs. The more money you get in scholarships, the less you'll have to work or borrow during school, and your life will be markedly easier upon graduation.

I have told students for years that **the single highest paying part-time job you could ever have in high school and college is applying for scholarships.** Imagine working for two hours on an application and essay for a $500 award from a local organization. Winning that award means you made $250 an hour! What if the scholarship was for $10,000? Can you imagine making $5,000 an hour while in high school?

I met Jessica at an event for high school students and she asked for advice about paying for college. She was thinking about attending an out-of-state private college, which had a tuition of $40,000 a year. "Here's the problem," she said. "My grades aren't *super* high. I'm a good student, probably in the top 10%, but not in the top 1%. Are there any awards I may be eligible for?"

I asked Jessica questions that seemed relevant to the scholarship search. Specifically, I asked her what her nationality was; she told me she was one fourth Japanese. I asked her what she was involved with in high school and she told me she was on the bowling team, played the clarinet in band, and participated in debate. I then asked her if she'd ever had any medical issues; she told me she has scoliosis (which is an abnormal curvature of the spine). I asked her about parents who are in the military, what she wanted to study and do for a living, as well as volunteer projects she'd been involved with. At this point, I had enough information to start searching.

When looking for scholarships for which to apply, Google is your best friend. The key is knowing how to search for the award opportunities. I started a Google search for Jessica by typing in "Japanese American Scholarships." The search resulted in 10 different award opportunities. Then, I searched "Female Bowling Scholarships," which produced 3,490,000 results (not all of them fit what we wanted, but at least 20 were awards for which Jessica could apply). I searched for scholarships related to clarinets, to debate, even to the top 10% of a class, and each of them resulted in awards for which Jessica could easily apply. Finally, I did searches for "Scoliosis Scholarships" and "Japanese American Scoliosis Scholarships." As crazy as it sounds, sometimes the combination of various topics (like females and bowling, or Japanese American and scoliosis) result in a more focused, direct search and tons of great opportunities. In Jessica's case, we quickly compiled a list of over 20 awards for which she was eligible.

Most students I speak to are unaware of the vast amount of awards offered in the local area alone. Because they are some of the easiest to apply for (and many come with a high likelihood of winning), I encourage you to look for awards from groups like: Kiwanis, Rotary, Jaycees, Lions Clubs, Optimist Club, Soroptimist Club, Knights of Columbus, local banks and credit unions, and any casinos in the state. The majority of these "civic organizations" that dole out scholarships require an application and *maybe* a short essay of 300-500 words. Trust me, you'll get to a point where you can bang out a scholarship essay in no time flat.

I've done over 400 hours of research into the scholarship process and boiled it all down into four videos you can access at www.MoneySavvy.com/ScholarshipMastery. The videos will walk you step-by-step through the process thousands of students have used to access millions of dollars worth of grants, awards, and other prizes. If you're new to the scholarship game, start with Video #1, follow the instructions, and see what happens.

Grants. Grants are similar to scholarships in that they don't have to be paid back. The most common grant, and one that many people are familiar with, is the Pell Grant. The Pell Grant is a program administered by the federal government whereby students with financial need from lower-income households are awarded an amount of money to help them cover the cost of tuition. While the amount you receive in a Pell Grant varies based on your financial need, the cost of attendance at your school, whether you're a full-time or part-time student, and how long you plan on attending, the *maximum* amount you can receive in Pell Grants is around $5,800 per year (based on 2016-2017 figures). This is not enough to cover even a semester of school at most state universities, so other ways and means of paying for school will have to be leveraged as well. To receive a grant, you (or more likely, your parents) will have to fill out a Free Application For Federal Student Aid, also known as the FAFSA. The FAFSA helps determine what your family's financial needs really are, which determines how much aid you'll be offered.

Work-study. Every college and university in the country offers some form of work-study where a student will work for the university, typically having to do with their chosen major, in exchange for funds to help cover the cost of their education. Work-study programs are valuable because you're not only helping cover the cost of your education, you're learning real-world skills in your field of expertise that add to your résumé. The amount of money/income you receive in work-study funds is in the $10 to $14 an hour range, depending on the school, program, and how much financial need you have based on the FAFSA. If you participate in a work-study program, keep in mind that every time you do the work, you've limited the amount of money you've borrowed to attend college!

Resident Assistant. The Resident Assistant, or RA, is the person responsible for overseeing the floor of a residence hall or dormitory. While this is typically only offered to a student once they've become a sophomore, the HUGE advantage is that RAs get all of their room and board for free. As of the time of this printing, the average cost of room and board is between $10,000 to $11,000 a year. If you were to take on this position for three years of your college career, you'd save yourself over $30,000. That equates to a payment of $330 for the next 10 years. RAs have been referred to as glorified babysitters; however, I've known students who take the RA position seriously and build skills in leadership, problem-solving, communication, and public speaking.

If you're attending a school where the cost of living is high, being an RA shields you from the expense of having to pay exorbitant rental costs. Your experience will vary based on the students living on your floor as well as the way you approach the position. Either way, the money you save by becoming a Resident Assistant is MASSIVE.

Advanced Placement Classes. AP (Advanced Placement) classes are higher level courses taken in high school that, at the end, allow a student to sit for a test to receive college credit. Typically, a minimum score must be achieved on the test to receive college credit, but universities around the world recognize the AP credits once achieved.

Let's assume the cost per credit hour at an average university is $500. Most classes are two or three credit hours (usually based on how many hours a week you're in class). That means for a three credit hour class, you'd pay $1,500. If you're taking an AP class while in high school, and you choose to take the test to get college credit, you'll pay a $90 testing fee. Pass the test and earn three credit hours, and you'll have saved $1,410. I've known students who have taken four or five AP classes before attending college. Using the numbers above, if these are three credit hour courses, a student who takes four AP tests and comes out with 12 hours of college credit has saved over $5,600 in college costs!

Community College Credit. If your high school is anywhere close to a community college, they more than likely have an agreement with the school district allowing you to take community college classes (as a high school student). The hours translate into college credits once you've finished the class. Typically offered to juniors and seniors in high school, these classes are held either during the day or at night, are on the community college campus or taught online, and the credits earned are transferable to a state or private college. Most students take general education requirements at the community college level so they can begin their major studies once they get to a four year school.

If you engineer this situation properly, it's possible to

graduate from high school and enter college as a second semester freshman or first semester sophomore. That would mean you've earned somewhere between 15 and 30 credit hours from community college courses. A total of 30 credit hours is considered a year of higher education. If you looked at the average cost of a year at a university, the savings are immense when you take college classes while in high school. You can save over $20,000 in pursuing your higher education degree.

CLEP Tests. CLEP, or College Level Examination Program, is a group of standardized tests created and administered by an organization known as The College Board. These tests gauge your level of understanding in various subjects, allowing you to receive college credit for what you've already learned. You may hear people say, "I've Clepped Out" of certain classes in college. This means they've taken a test in American History or Accounting or any of over 30 other classes, passed, and received college credit for already knowing the information. The CLEP test costs $80, and The College Board offers a variety of products and services to help you prepare for taking the test.

Most students either have little knowledge of the CLEP opportunity or tell themselves, "I'm no good at taking tests anyway, so what's the use?" If you were to put a little effort into studying before taking the test, you may save yourself $1,500 on one class. Do that a handful of times and you've minimized the cost of college exponentially. Find out more about the opportunities CLEP provides at www.MoneySavvy.com/CLEP.

Community College Degree. For some students, there is a stigma around attending a community college versus a state or private four year school. Let me dispel this and give you some context around community colleges across the country.

Community colleges have long been known as places to go to prepare for vocational or technical work. Often there was a negative connotation to attending community college because the person "didn't know what they wanted to do." I believe starting your career at a community college is one of the most Money Savvy things you can do. The number of students who drop out after their first year of school is staggering—30% as of the date of this printing.[4] In my opinion, there is no better way to put your toe in the water of higher education without incurring a mountain of debt.

Community colleges are not only one of the greatest values in pursuing higher education, but they prepare students for actual work in the real world. There are programs in telephony, laser technology, nursing, welding, airplane maintenance, and hundreds of other fields that are hiring and in constant need of new workers. One of my close friends is a provost at a community college and tells me he gets calls daily asking for graduates of certain programs, like network technology and welding. These are jobs that pay $40,000-$50,000 a year, and they can't find enough qualified candidates. Keep in mind that in our country we graduate nearly four million college students a year, but only create around two million jobs annually.[5]

A student who receives a degree from a community college in a field which hires directly from the program has several things going for them:

First, they *know* the degree they received has an ROI (Return On Investment). A community college nearby has a laser technology program that lasts 18 months, costs $12,000 to attend, and their graduates are getting job offers in the $70,000 to $80,000 range. That is a solid ROI.

Second, having solid job prospects gives them the ability to test the market and see if they like what they're doing. I can't tell you how many students go to school for four, five, six, or more years, then realize they HATE the field of study they chose. The problem was they never had any real-life experience in the field. Some graduate with a specific degree only to realize that industry isn't hiring. Many community college programs are directly in-line with current hiring trends, meaning there are jobs waiting for graduates of those programs.

Third, the amount of debt they've taken on is minimal. There should be no concern as to their ability to pay back the money borrowed, especially if they're Money Savvy!

Lastly, community college grads can take their associate's degree to virtually any other school and enter as a junior. Most state schools have agreements with community colleges allowing two year degree credits to transfer in. By doing this, you'll save in the neighborhood of $30,000 to $40,000 in tuition, room, board, and fees the first two years.

Employer Programs. In June 2014, Starbucks was the first public company to announce they would launch a College Achievement Plan, a company-wide offering that enabled employees (full- and part-time, working 20 hours or more) to attend Arizona State University with full tuition coverage. ASU, in partnership with Starbucks, created an online degree program that allows the coffee company employees to take classes from anywhere when it's convenient for them.[6] Starbucks may have been the first, but there will be many companies that follow suit. In your quest to graduate college with as little debt as possible, consider looking at companies that have either a tuition help program or debt repayment programs as a benefit to working there.

The Military. This suggestion often conjures up a "boots on the ground" image, but the reality is that the U.S. Military needs people of all kinds to help keep their operations running smoothly. No matter which branch of the military may interest you, every base has jobs that don't always involve carrying a gun or being on the front line. They need logistics people, HR professionals, mechanics, chefs, dentists, IT professionals, radar engineers—the list could go on and on. The key is to identify what you see yourself doing

and follow that path while serving in the military. The benefits are amazing and are worth investigating if you're at all
interested in having school costs covered this way.

The Montgomery G.I. Bill offers educational financial
assistance whether you're on Active Duty or enlisted in the
National Guard or Reserves. Find out more information at
http://www.benefits.va.gov/gibill.

What's Your Strategy?

Given today's costs of attending school, the bottom line is
this is a business decision. As with any business decision, it's
important to have a strategy in place as to how you'll get the
best return from your investment. Armed with no plan and
no financial understanding, you are automatically signing up
for decades of debt repayment (unless your parents have been
VERY diligent about investing, you are a master of the scholarship game, or your grades and test scores are incredible).

At the very least, part of your strategy should include
how to get as much college credit as possible while still in
high school. Those "free" credit hours from the local community college represent real dollars you won't have to spend
taking classes at the university level. That, in and of itself, is
money in the bank.

As a next step, I encourage you to apply for at least
five-ten scholarships before you graduate from high school.
Applying once or twice and throwing in the towel doesn't
work. Until you've got at least three solid essays under your
belt, you're just a beginner. If you want to be a master, take

this on as a part-time job.

Listen, I LOVED my college experience. I think it's the greatest four years of a person's life if done right. I also think four years of college can cause 20 years or more of financial distress because your prefrontal cortex isn't in place yet.

If College Isn't Your Thing

Admitting to the fact that you don't see yourself in college right now can be very challenging in today's society. For the past several decades, we've made college an absolute for those finishing high school. Ask nearly any educator from any grade what they're doing in their classroom and they'll tell you, "We're preparing our students for college." That's not a bad thing, especially when a high percentage of job openings require a bachelor's degree. But, if you don't want to spend the next four years studying, writing, and sitting in class, what will become of you? I believe you have plenty of options, IF you decide to go about it with a strategy.

Apprenticeships. Dating back to the Middle Ages, apprenticeships were used to train the next generation of craftsmen, builders, bakers, blacksmiths, and virtually every other position that a community needed to thrive. Had there been no one to pass the work down to, a lack of leadership in critical functions (like baking and blacksmithing) would have led to breakdowns in society.

Today, the idea of an apprenticeship is as alive and well

as it ever has been, but the stigma associated with it leaves people passing over the opportunity when they should be looking at it intently. Apprenticeships are offered in every union oriented trade, like steamfitters, sheet metal, timber framers, plumbers, and electricians. While there are *many* advantages to apprenticeships, the greatest is the fact that you earn while you learn.

At the core of the apprenticeship is learning your trade, moving through the apprenticeship ranks until you become a journeyman, and eventually graduating to proficient status. All the while as you're learning the trade, you're making better-than-average money, taking classes, and getting practice. You'll work with various professionals who will teach you how to succeed in the industry, and in the end, come out of the three to four year process making great money, typically in the $60,000 range.

Online and Immersion Courses. The sheer amount of education you can access online is staggering, whether you're accessing these "courses" from free sites like KhanAcademy.org, Lynda.com, or YouTube.com, OR you're leveraging the courses that you can purchase on Udemy.com or Udacity.com. For that matter you can log onto Edx.com, Coursera.com, or take classes from schools like Harvard and Stanford—all online and mostly free.

The example I'm most fond of is a company called Code Academy. On their website Codecademy.com, they claim you can "Learn to code interactively, for free." Before writing this book, I investigated the viability of someone who goes through Code Academy getting a decent job. One of my good friends who runs a start-up in Silicon Valley said he regularly hires people who don't have a degree but have plenty of coursework through Code Academy. He went so far as to tell me he'd *rather* hire them over someone with a Management Information Systems (MIS) degree because they:

a) Are generally self-taught or at least self-paced, and therefore learn new things easily.

b) Aren't bogged down learning outdated coding systems and instead are nimble, creative, and up-to-date on the latest programming languages.

One of the main differences between online or immersion classes and traditional higher education is instead of studying a variety of topics over a number of years, you're more than likely digging deep into your main course of study much faster. An immersion course may have you up and running in your expertise within weeks or months instead of years. Another major difference between immersion classes and traditional higher education tracks is that colleges and universities have to wait for accreditation or approval of the subject and materials before they can teach the latest technology. This often puts their curriculum months if not years behind the latest innovations.

Job Shadowing. A young woman I met about a year ago was considering going to school for graphic design when a mutual friend intervened. Drew owns a marketing firm and invited this young lady into his company to work in an administrative role about 70% of the time, with 30% of her time devoted to working alongside his graphic design team. His advice to her was if she was interested in learning about art, better to work around it as close to full-time as possible, instead of studying it part-time for years.

Within one year of her employment, Drew had promoted her to an Associate Graphic Designer role with expanded responsibilities and significant client interaction— experience she was only getting because of her earlier job shadowing opportunity. Had she opted for a more traditional higher education path, she would've spent the first year taking general education requirements and might just now be learning actual graphic design.

Make no mistake, pursuing a job shadow requires that you work hard, you show up ready to learn, and you invest in yourself. Don't be surprised if you have to work your way into the career you're looking to establish. Trust in the fact there is *always* someone willing to provide you an opportunity.

What if I Have No Idea What I Want To Do for a Living?

Here's the good news: You're not alone. There are people two or three times your age who still have no idea what they want to do for a living. However, there's a big difference between not knowing and not trying to figure it out. There are several ways for you to investigate viable options before you commit to tens of thousands of dollars in tuition. Here are a few:

Informational Interviewing. As you think about what you want to do for a living, seek out the individuals who are already performing those jobs. Get in touch with them and ask if you can take them to coffee to learn more about their daily lives at work. The goal is to find out what they like or dislike about their career, what got them to where they are, any missteps they took along the way, and what they recommend for a young person starting out. Here's the key: use the "I'm a student" all-access pass. By reaching out and letting them know you're a student trying to find your way in this world, they'll be much more open to sitting down and giving you 30 minutes of their time.

Shadowing. One of my good friends is in the top 10% of all realtors in the state. He's been in the business for about 10 years, and in the past five he has crushed it. He always has someone shadowing him who is interested in getting into real estate. Some are recent college grads, some seasoned professionals looking for a career change, and a handful have been high school students thinking about pursuing real estate in lieu of college. Being an expert in the business, he's a great guy to model, and by shadowing him all of these people get a sense of whether they would like the business. One or two days of shadowing may be all you need to say, "Yep, that's for me," or "No way do I see myself doing that."

Mentorship. Much like an apprenticeship, mentorship is

when someone more seasoned or experienced guides someone with less experience. Having a mentor is critical when you're faced with life-altering decisions. Ideally, your mentor has been through something similar and can lead you through the thought processes to make the most appropriate decision. Finding a mentor can often be a challenge, but I encourage you to ask your family, friends, teachers, and peers who they think would be good for you in that role. Oftentimes, someone close to you is serving as your mentor and you didn't even realize it. Don't overlook close family, but don't count on your family to know what's best for you, either.

Assessments. If you're more comfortable figuring things out on your own instead of working with others, perhaps a number of assessments is best for you. Various assessments will tell you what your aptitudes are, what your social style is, how you learn best, and in what career you might excel. The following link lists assessments that may help you in figuring out who you want to be when you "grow up:" www.MoneySavvy.com/CareerPath.

Experiment. There is nothing wrong with "kicking the tires" of a job or career to see if you like it. So much fuss is made of job-hopping, yet until and unless you get experience in an industry, how will you ever know if you like it? Think about conducting mini-experiments within industries. Take six months at a time and test a bunch of different environments to see what you like. Again, using the "I'm just a student" all-access pass, you will get your foot in the door as an intern getting valuable experience before deciding what it is you want to do for the rest of your life. Side note: The "rest of your life" rarely happens in today's society. People are expected to have four to five different *careers* in their lifetime. Not jobs. Careers.

The famous Chinese philosopher Confucius once said, "Choose a job you love, and you will never work a day in your life." How are you supposed to know what you love until you experience the people, the environment, or at least a bit of the work? By choosing a few of the above methods, you'll get a better sense of what kind of work appeals to you, what fuels your passion, and what could fit the "Never work a day in your life" ideal. I've known students who blaze into college having never done this kind of searching, spend four to five years on a course of study, and then realize it isn't what fires them up. I've known students who have started school, studied for a couple of years, and then left to find their passions in the world, only to return more passionate about school than they'd ever been. And, I've known students who realize their passions and begin making money straight away, forgoing traditional higher education altogether.

The secret is: **There is no ONE right path.** The path you take is up to you. Oftentimes, there are only one or two paths illuminated for you, making the rest seem rather daunting. The benefit you have is that you are becoming a Money Savvy Student and life is always easier for them.

Make hard choices and life is easy; make easy choices and life is hard.

MAKING IT RAIN

When I was eight years old, my mom taught me how to bake a cake off the side of the Hershey's cocoa can. While I now realize she was stroking my ego, at the time she made me think I had baked the *greatest cake in the history of cakes*. I was so convinced of my extraordinary baking ability that I set about building a "cake cart" that I would use to cart these cakes throughout the neighborhood, peddling them door-to-door. Two very gracious neighbors agreed to buy my high-end chocolate cakes for eight dollars a piece and I thought I was rich. Mom later told me they were skeptical of how good the cake may or may not be, but I was a closer and they were enamored by my childlike entrepreneurialism. The hardest lesson came when my Dad took out the cost of what it took to make the cake; he said I needed to learn what the word profit meant (Revenue - Costs = Profit).

My entrepreneurial tendencies followed me throughout

grade school, middle school, junior high, high school, college, and well into my working life. In middle school I sold candy out of my locker; in junior high and high school I was paid to play taps on my trumpet at the funerals of war veterans; in college I invested in giant popcorn vending machines I placed all over town, I sold books door-to-door during the summers, and DJ'd dances on weekends. Today, I consider myself "functionally unemployable" by someone else. It's not that I can't get a job – I get offers on a regular basis. It's that I don't *want* a job.

I've been selling things since I was a kid and was enamored by the ability to make money from something as simple as an idea. If you're like-minded in any way, you're going to love this chapter. Most students I speak with on high school and college campuses will tell me they need a job. My line of questioning goes something like this: How much can you make part-time per hour? How many hours a week do you have to work? Have you considered how much will be deducted in taxes? Have you ever thought about…?

When all you have is a hammer, everything looks like a nail.

Our school system was set up a century ago and not much has changed. While the delivery of content may have advanced with technology, it seems the outcome of the system itself has not. In the early 1900s, we were an industrialized nation with the need for literate factory workers. Our public school system was engineered to be a factory for pumping out people who could go punch clocks and work on assembly lines. The difference today is graduates are pumped out and pushed to college, where they're supposed to be educated to be part of the workforce.

Did you catch that? Part of the workforce. Not owners, not entrepreneurs – part of the workforce. Now, I'm not saying being part of the workforce is bad – in fact, I was a part of the workforce for the first eight or nine years of my post-college life. But, the statistics today suggest that by the year 2020, close to half of our population will be independent contractors.[1] That means they'll rely on entrepreneurship to make it. It means instead of having one employer, you might have five or 10 or 15 clients. Unfortunately, we're still engineering students to think, "I have to get a job." My fear is that if you aren't even *aware* of the entrepreneurial potential out there, you'll miss the boat.

Real Life Entrepreneurs

There is nothing I like more than a great entrepreneurial success story. Because a great portion of my speaking is done around the topic, people share these stories with me all the time. What I've come to understand is that most people have no idea these kinds of businesses exist or what people make through their business. The following section is designed to give you inspiration, hope for what's possible, and a kick in the seat to try something entrepreneurial!

$75,000 A Year Mowing Lawns In College

David borrowed $1,000 from his parents to invest in a John Deere riding lawn mower when he was 16. It was one of those zero-turn radius mowers that doesn't have a steering wheel but instead has two handles you pull forward or backward to drive and steer. Bought brand new, David would've paid over $3,000 for this machine, but he found a great deal on Craigslist and negotiated the mower down to $1,000.

Within the first month of owning the mower, David secured eight homes in his neighborhood for mowing services and charged them $35 each to mow their yards once per week. He paid his parents back in the first month *and* had cash to spare.

When it was time for David to go to college, his Dad encouraged him to take the mower to school with him and continue the business in the small town where his private college was located. He found a nice elderly lady with an empty garage stall and he mowed her lawn in exchange for keeping the mower on her property. Then, he built a substantially larger base of clients in the college town than he had at home. In no time, David was covering the tuition on his own using mowing revenue.

During David's sophomore year, he took a business class where one of the assignments was to write a business plan. Because he already had a business, he used his own company as the basis for the plan. His professor asked David to see him after class one day and told him the college had put out a bid request for landscaping and mowing services around campus. David said, "I'm only one guy with one mower." His professor's response was, "You are one guy with one mower, but your business plan calls for a fleet of trucks, mowers, snow-plowing, and various landscaping services. If you bid this project, your business may have to expand to fit your plan."

Encouraged by his professor's belief in his vision, David submitted a quote for landscaping services at the college. He cited his growing list of clients in the community, many of whom either taught or worked at the school. After an interview and a few slight revisions to the bid, David was awarded the project and began building out his company to provide services to the campus.

Fast forward to David's senior year. He owns three pickup trucks, each with their own trailer pulling two mowers. He employs seven of his fraternity buddies who mow during the spring and summer and push snow in the winter. Their crew maintains the campus and the grounds of multiple apartment complexes in the city and surrounding area, and David makes $75,000 a year and has a net worth of over $300,000.

David is a Money Savvy Student!

$900 In One Day With $12 in Supplies

Sean was a student on the East Coast when I first met him. He was a senior in high school and came from a family that did not make enough money to help him cover the costs of attending college. Sean knew he would have to take out

loans, but was nervous about what that meant after graduation—after all, he saw at home that debt caused problems,
fear, and arguments.

"Would you be open to a crazy idea that requires a very
small investment, a fair amount of work, and will make you
more money in one day than you can currently imagine?" I
asked Sean.

"I'm all ears," was Sean's response.

I told him that I think one of the most overlooked businesses for young people today is washing windows. It's a job
I absolutely detest doing at home, yet about twice a year my
wife has me up on a ladder, making sure our windows are
sparkly clean.

"For the price of a bucket from The Home Depot, a
squeegee, and a few rags, you can be in business. I bet you
can buy all of that for less than $12. Then, go borrow a ladder
from someone and you're in business," I told him.

Sean and his crew were all nodding their heads, but deep
down I never believed they'd do anything with the information. Imagine my surprise when, about six months later, Sean
sent me a message saying he and a couple of friends launched
their business and made $900 in one day. He included a link
to their Facebook page promoting their window washing business for high-end homes and businesses.

When I asked Sean how they made their money, he told
me they went to an affluent neighborhood and went door-to-
door, asking residents if they'd like their windows washed
on the outside of their home. If no one was home, they left a
flyer describing their services, letting the homeowner know

they'd be in the area all day. Once they started on a few homes, people began driving by and shouting out their address, asking the guys to come by. All in all, he said, they cleaned the windows of 12 homes that day and made $900.

Sean told me he was no longer concerned about where he would get the money he needed for school. It was as if he'd cleared a mental hurdle—the one placed squarely in front of people who believe, "If I want to make money, I have to find a job."

Feed Your Social Media Addiction—And Your Wallet

Lindsay is a student at a large state university in Pennsylvania who I met through an event I did on her campus. She's a brilliant student, studies marketing and PR, and lives for her major. You could honestly say she found her passion and will most likely never "work" another day in her life.

The event that Lindsay helped market and promote had the highest number of attendees of any event ever held on campus. She dominated the social media aspect of promoting the event, leveraging various aspects of social media that had never occurred to me. I was blown away to have nearly 5% of the entire campus in this ballroom when I showed up to present, thanks to the promotions team, and primarily Lindsay.

After the event we did a quick download of the success of the event and the logistics behind the attendance. Lindsay shared her strategies and told me she was doing similar work for a number of clients.

"What sort of clients are you working with?" I asked her.

"All types. Everything from bars and restaurants to flower shops and auto detailers."

Super intrigued by this super-entrepreneur, I asked her how she built her business while attending school and what she saw happening in the future.

"The business built itself—I was doing social media for a friend's bar and word started to spread about the success of the campaigns I was running. Really basic stuff like drink specials and theme nights, but I was putting it all over Facebook, Twitter, Instagram, and Snapchat. The owner referred me to a few people, and that grew into what it is today."

All told, Lindsay had seven clients paying her a guaranteed amount of money every month as a social media management fee. She offered them various packages which involved getting them set up on Google Places, YouTube, Facebook, Twitter, Snapchat, and Instagram. For added fees, she'd help them build a mailing list of frequent clients, allowing them to do more direct marketing. After several months of working with her clients, they almost always asked for more help. Her average monthly revenue per client was $350, but spiked as high as $1,000 depending on their needs.

When I asked her how she juggled work and attending school full-time, she told me a couple of her friends were short on cash so she hired them as independent contractors to manage some of the posts or create images for Instagram.

"It's a total win-win," she said. "They get to work when it's convenient for them, and I get to deliver amazing results to my clients. I figure I'll either sell the business when I'm done with school or build it into a digital agency that will become my full-time gig."

Lindsay tapped into **one of the greatest secrets in business—recurring revenue.** All she needs to do is sell the service once, deliver great results, and the revenue will continue for the foreseeable future. If you take one thing from this book, Money Savvy Students think in terms of recurring revenue!

$200 A Week Taking Walks

Jess was home from college on break and overheard the neighbor talking about her son struggling in Spanish. She offered to help him with vocabulary and some conversational phrases while she was home, and the neighbor gratefully accepted. The next day, Jess and the neighbor's kid, an 8th grader, went for a walk. Jess taught him nouns in Spanish by pointing things out on the walk. They did this for an hour or so each day, four days in a row. Every day, Jess taught new words, throwing in some additional sentence structure and pronunciation lessons, until she went back to school. On the last "Spanish Walk" as she called them, the neighbor handed Jess a $100 bill.

Jess did the math on the way home from the neighbors and realized she'd just made $25 an hour. Surely there were families like this one back at school that would hire her to do similar work with their kids. She placed a simple ad on Craigslist detailing services as a Spanish tutor for kids in

6th-12th grade. She fielded a number of requests from people asking about her service before she landed her first client. A very nice family hired her to tutor their 11th grade daughter one to two hours per week, depending on her progress.

Leveraging the success of the "Spanish Walk," Jess had worked with this student for about three weeks when she received requests from other students in the same class. She learned her original student was raving about her and how much fun they had learning the language while walking around the neighborhood.

At the height of her business, Jess was averaging about $200 per week taking walks and speaking Spanish with eager students.

What skill or ability do you have that could be leveraged for additional income? I shared this story with a young friend of mine named Jeff. Jeff was a sophomore when I first met him. He told me there wasn't anything he could teach to make extra money, and knowing his background, I challenged him.

"So, there's nothing you could teach?" I asked.

"Nothing I'd feel comfortable being an expert in," Jeff replied.

I happened to know that Jeff had bowled five perfect games in his short life, a feat not many people can claim.

"Could you teach me how to throw a bowling ball so it backspins like the pros?" I asked.

"Of course, but that's different," he said.

"You're telling me that there aren't bowling teams that

would pay you $75 to $100 to hang out with them on league night and coach their every throw?"

After a little convincing, Jeff spent Wednesday nights at the local bowling alley, hired by various teams to be their "bowling coach" for the evening. It was extra pocket cash for Jeff and he had a blast doing it.

See For Yourself—A Challenge

Craigslist.com has to be one of the greatest things to happen to society in the past 20 years (and yes, it's over 20 years old!). If you want to test out your entrepreneurial abilities, I'm issuing you a challenge that's easy to do, takes little time, and will prove to you how easy it is to make money today.

First, understand that Craigslist.com is a great site because you can find nearly anything for sale. But, what makes it even greater is the fact that people who are selling stuff are TERRIBLE at writing product descriptions that really sell the reader. Have you ever read the posts on CraigsList? The majority of them are *awful*.

So, here's the challenge:

1. Find something to buy or pick up for free on CraigsList. Make sure that whatever you're getting has some value (nothing broken or trashy). Small pieces of furniture like end tables, chairs, or small chests work wonderfully. If you can get it for free, this challenge is a piece of cake. If you are paying for it, just make sure you're getting a bargain!

2. Write NEW marketing copy (which is just a glorified way of saying a product description) that absolutely sizzles! Write it in a way that someone who reads it will think, "I have to have this." Exercise your creative energy, write and rewrite it, then show it to someone for their opinion.

3. Sell the item for a profit. Whether that's double the price or an additional $10 or $20 over what you paid, it doesn't matter. The key is taking something that's not marketed well, buying it, and selling it for more than you paid for it.

If you get good at this, you could fund about anything your heart desires. I know students who pay their way through school doing CraigsList buying and selling. Ryan Finlay started a business buying and selling appliances on CraigsList. He did it so well, after a few years he moved his family to Hawaii full-time and now teaches others how to build businesses doing the same thing. You can find him at: http://recraigslist.com.

The New Digital Frontier of Making Money

We are living in one of the most amazing ages when it comes to technology and business. In the past 10 years, the number of tech start-ups, app companies, bot companies, and various other ways of generating revenue in non-traditional ways has exploded. The youngest self-made billionaire in the world is

24 (Evan Spiegel of Snapchat).

And yet, when I discuss business and entrepreneurship with students, I'm amazed that they're not familiar with sites, apps, opportunities, and tools being used to build businesses by young people around the globe. The following list is full of ideas, tools, and resources you should know about.

Amazon.com. Yes, you probably know about Amazon and have no doubt ordered from this incredible company. But, did you know that Amazon has absolutely leveled the playing field when it comes to starting a business? Anyone can open an Amazon storefront, anyone can publish books on the Kindle Desktop Publishing platform or use Print On Demand services from Createspace.com (an Amazon company). Amazon is the gold rush of your generation! Simply Google search: "Making money on Amazon" and see how many posts come up.

YouTube.com. You've wasted hours, days, maybe even weeks of your life watching YouTube videos. Did you know there are people raking in profits by creating YouTube channels, developing a following, and earning revenue off the advertising that plays before the clip? Check out the guys from Dude Perfect, a trick shot team of college buddies who hang out all day and make epic basketball long shots. They now have their own line of NERF products and a show on the CMT Network. There's a kid who does nothing but make paper airplanes, ninja stars, and other origami paper products who made well over six figures last year from his clips. There are people who do nothing but play video games, record the video with their commentary, and profit from the ad revenue. Are you intrigued?

Gumroad.com. This site allows creative types to sell their products and services with the click of a button. There is no simpler way to create something and then turn around and sell it. Are you a photographer? Artist? Author? Want to teach people how to do something? This is how you sell it to the masses.

Paypal.com. Still one of the best ways on the Internet to transfer money, pay for stuff, or collect from those who owe you. Paypal allows you to create customized buttons that embed on a website or in email so someone can pay for your services automatically, online, and with little hassle.

Shopify.com. Build an online store for the products you create with a few clicks of a mouse. Shopify allows you to have your very own storefront online with all of your products and merchandise on sale 24/7/365.

Mailchimp.com. One of the easiest sites to build an email list of people who want to hear from you, Mailchimp captures email addresses from your website. It then automates the responses to those contacts in a simple-to-setup process.

Craigslist.com. For reasons already covered, CraigsList is a virtual goldmine of treasures and profit. Get REALLY good at writing creative sales copy and this will be your favorite site.

Wordpress.com. Want to build a following through your writing, artwork, videos, or ideas on your own site? Make sure you're building your site on a WordPress template.

Canva.com. This site allows you to make your own professionally designed images for social media – just in case you want to start your own social media marketing firm.

99Designs.com. Don't know how to design a logo, website, company brand, etc.? Have no fear, just run a contest on 99Designs, a site with multiple designers competing for the work. The results are incredible and the cost is minimal compared to hiring someone to build out a logo for you individually.

Upwork.com. Hiring a freelancer (or a team of them) has never been easier. Upwork.com is the go-to site if you want to hire someone from around the world to help you with a project or idea. Whether you need someone to research, design, develop an app, code, or write, they're all here and ready to work for you at prices so low it's almost hard to believe. As an example, I hired a woman in the Philippines to do research for a project. She did 100 hours of research and charged me $400. That's four dollars an hour—and she had a Ph.D. from an American University!

If you want to learn how to make money online, you probably won't learn it in school. Famed business philosopher Jim Rohn used to say, "Formal education will make you a living. Self education will make you a fortune." Study the sites above and research other people who've built their incomes using these tools. The more you test and play around with any of these sites, the more likely (and rapid) your success!

The Rise of Crowdfunding

Typically, the largest barrier to entry to starting a business, project, or passion is the money to make it happen. However, technology today has closed the gap between an amazing idea and the money to bring it to fruition. In the past 15 years, crowdfunding has exploded and is used to launch companies, films, musicians, products, books, and everything else you can imagine.

The idea of crowdfunding is simple: propose an idea to a group of enthusiasts, point them to a website that allows for the collection of funds to make your dream a reality, and execute on your idea.

Companies have sprung up overnight when their crowdfunding campaigns went viral, raising millions of dollars when all they asked for was several thousand. Crowdfunding has created ridiculous campaigns like the guy who wanted to raise money to make the most delicious potato salad and ended up with $55,000.[2] Candidly, I gave $10 to this potato salad guy because I thought it was a clever idea.

In 2014, I crowdfunded a documentary project on the student loan debt issue in America and raised $67,000 in 45 days. The film is called *Broke, Busted, & Disgusted* and is on its way to Netflix at the time of this writing. We're getting picked up by a handful of cable networks—all because of the power of crowdfunding.

The point of this section is to encourage you to test your ideas. No one asked me if I had a background in documentaries. No one challenged me or my ability to tell a story or finish my product. Crowdfunding allows you to deliver on an idea without having to jump through the hoops that you would've 20 years ago to prove you're worth the risk to investors. Here are the sites you need to know about:

www.Kickstarter.com

www.Indiegogo.com

www.GoFundMe.com

Your Timing Is Perfect

There has never been another time in history as perfect as this one for making it rain. Hopefully you can see the entrepreneurial landscape has been leveled for you, IF you put forth the effort. When teenagers turn into billionaires within 10 years, you should be inspired that you have the same potential given the amazing technological advances and education available for next to nothing.

The key is trying, failing, trying, failing, and continuing the try and fail process until you master what it is you're attempting to do. It's how every successful entrepreneur before you has done it. Not knowing how is no longer a good reason not to try—there are far too many ways to bring your ideas to fruition.

Most important of all, I want you to take from this chapter the knowledge that having a job is not the only way to make money, it is simply ONE way to make money. Once you lock into the idea that you can make money in a multitude of ways, independently from anyone else, you'll have no trouble making it rain!

YOUR NEXT STEPS TO
BECOMING MONEY SAVVY

First, let me congratulate you for making it this far in the book. I once heard that the average college graduate only reads 0.9 books a year! 0.9! Not even one whole book. I'd say you've blown past the 0.9 mark, so congratulations!

By reading this book, you're already closer to being Money Savvy. However, as you know by now, it's not just about knowing, it's about doing. There are millions of people in this world who know *how* to do something, they just aren't *doing* it. So, taking the information from the book, there are a few things you can do from here:

1. **Create a realistic budget:** I can guarantee that if you have no idea how much is coming in and going out, you're overspending. Only those who

operate from a budget can leverage their highest Money Savvy Habits.

2. **Set up your emergency fund of at least $500:** This is critical, even if you have to stop spending for a few weeks to do it. Once you've put that amount away, you'll feel secure, abundant, and ready to tackle the next steps in building your wealth.

3. **Study and KNOW the Basics:** Your understanding of the basics, like income, expenses, debt, insurance, taxes, stocks, bonds, investments, compounding, etc. is the key to making informed choices when it comes to money. That new car you want? Is it the best decision financially? You'll know how to make that assessment if you understand the basics of Savvy finances.

4. **Investigate college costs and funding options:** Graduate from college with as little debt as possible while attaining your educational goals. This means applying for scholarships like it's your job, getting credits for college in high school, and looking at the alternatives to expensive paths. If college isn't for you, have that conversation as early as possible and begin exploring alternative paths.

5. **Research industries, careers, and jobs you may enjoy:** You'll make far more money in your life if you love what you do. Do some of that searching now while you have time.

6. **Make it rain:** What can you do *right now* to make money that doesn't have you behind a counter for $9 an hour? Use your creativity, your talent, your current skills, your ability to delegate – whatever it takes to prove that you have an entrepreneur in you. You may need it someday. There's no better time than when you're young to test your ability to make money on your own.

7. **CONTINUE LEARNING:** This is just the beginning. Grab any and all books on financial topics and I promise you they'll change your life. You can find a list of recommended reading here: www.Money Savvy.com/MoneyBooks

I've been asked why I chose to write this book and there are a number of reasons. My first book, *Winning The Money Game*, which is used by high schools and colleges across the country, needed an update. It was originally written in 2005 and there have been incredible changes since then. The founder of Snapchat was 13 when I wrote it and today he's a billionaire. YouTube was just founded, smartphones just introduced, social media was still MySpace and Bebo (you had to be there). The bottom line is that our economy is changing faster than ever and only those in the know will keep up.

I regularly meet college graduates and people in their 30s who don't understand basic financial concepts. Financial education *has got* to start earlier in life before irreparable decisions are made. Forgive the doom and gloom, but I'd rather be real with you. Your generation will make or break this economy.

Listen, your elders have done a horrible job of preparing a better future for you. There are massive amounts of debt in our society, unrealistic unemployment, and we've told your generation to "trust the system." The positive reality is that there are still incredible opportunities awaiting you. We need you to care, to know better, and to be ready to act differently than previous generations. In short, **I think you're part of the solution.**

The real reason I wrote this book is that I believe your generation gives society a chance to reboot. A chance to figure things out with fresh eyes. Albert Einstein once said, "You can't solve a problem with the same level of thinking that created it." The level of thinking that created the current economic situation came from people who didn't get financially educated until it was too late. That's how life works differently than school—in school you get the lesson first and the test second; in life you get the test first and the lesson second. We can't afford to let you fail the test to learn the lesson. Literally. We can't afford for you to fail.

I made a bold prediction at the beginning of the book that if you take the information seriously, it will radically change your life. Standing by that prediction, I'll leave you with a question:

Are you serious about becoming Money Savvy? Then get after it.

NOTES

Chapter Two:

1. Hicken, Melanie. (2014, August 18) *Average Cost of Raising A Child Hits $245,000.* Retrieved from http://money.cnn.com/2014/08/18/pf/child-cost, May 5, 2016.

Chapter Four:

1. Berman, Nat. (2016, June) *How Shaquille O'Neal Became a Successful Entrepreneur.* Retrieved from http://moneyinc.com/shaquille-oneal-entrepreneur, May 5th 2016.

Chapter Six:

1. Pofelt, Elaine. (2012, April 3) *What You'll Need To Know To Be The Boss in 2020.* Retrieved from http://www.forbes.com/sites/elainepofeldt/2012/04/03/what-youll-need-to-know-to-be-the-boss-in-2020/#62bb5d032f34, July 6, 2016.

Chapter Seven:

1. Peterson, Lars. (2014, October 15) *The Notebook That Will Change How You Think About Money Forever.* Retrieved from http://money. usnews.com/money/blogs/my-money/2014/10/15/the-notebook-that-will-change-how-you-think-about-money-forever, July 6, 2016.

Chapter Ten:

1. US Debt Clock. Retrieved from http://www.usdebtclock.org, May 5, 2016.

2. Street, Chriss W. (2015, April 15) *Study: Over 27% of Student Loans Are In Default.* Retrieved from http://www.breitbart.com/big-government/2015/04/15/study-over-27-of-student-loans-are-in-default/, July 6, 2016.

Chapter Eleven:

1. Ladika, Susan. (2011, August 23) *A Parent's Guide To Insurance For Teen Drivers.* Retrieved from http://www.carinsurance.com/Articles/best-ways-to-insure-teen-driver.aspx?WT.qs_osrc=fxb-20102610, May 5, 2016.

Chapter Twelve:

1. Woodruff, Judy. (2008, September 5) *How Do We Fund Our Schools?* Retrieved from http://www.pbs.org/wnet/wherewestand/reports/finance/how-do-we-fund-our-schools/?p=197, May 9, 2016.

2. Pomerleau, Kyle. (2015, October 14) *2016 Tax Brackets.* Retrieved from http://taxfoundation.org/article/2016-tax-brackets, May 9, 2016.

Chapter Thirteen:

1. Average Starting Teacher Salaries By State. Retrieved from http://www.nea.org/home/2012-2013-average-starting-teacher-salary.html, April 26, 2016.

2. *Entry Level Mechanical Engineer Salary United States.* Retrieved from http://www.payscale.com/research/US/Job=Mechanical_Engineer/Salary/5b1f9aef/Entry-Level, April 26, 2016.

3. The College Board, Annual Survey of Colleges. *Average Estimated Undergraduate Budgets, 2015-2016.* Retrieved from https://trends.collegeboard.org/college-pricing/figures-tables/average-estimated-undergraduate-budgets-2015-16, July 10, 2016.

4. Beckstead, Rachel. (2015, October 14) *College Dropout Statistics.* Retrieved from http://www.collegeatlas.org/college-dropout.html, July 10, 2016.

5. National Center For Education Statistics. *Back To School Statistics.* Retrieved from http://nces.ed.gov/fastfacts/display.asp?id=372, July 10, 2016.

6. Starbucks Newsroom. *Starbucks College Achievement Plan: Frequently Asked Questions.* Retrieved from https://news.starbucks.com/views/starbucks-college-achievement-plan-frequently-asked-questions, April 28, 2016.

Chapter Fifteen:

1. Schrader, Brendon. (2015, August 10) *Here's Why The Freelancer Economy Is On The Rise.* Retrieved from http://www.fastcompany.com/3049532/the-future-of-work/heres-why-the-freelancer-economy-is-on-the-rise, July 9, 2016.

2. Brown, Zack. *Danger. I'm Making Potato Salad.* Retrieved from https://www.kickstarter.com/projects/zackdangerbrown/potato-salad, August 12, 2016.